# THE LORD IS MY SHEPHERD

D1102246

# The Lord Is My Shepherd

David E. Rosage

SERVANT BOOKS
Ann Arbor, Michigan

Copyright © 1984 by David E. Rosage
All rights reserved

Published by Servant Books
P.O. Box 8617
Ann Arbor, Michigan 48107

Cover Photo: John Colwell from Grant Heilman
Book design by John B. Leidy

Psalm texts are © The Grail (England) 1963
and published by Collins, London, 1963. Used with
permission.

Printed in the United States of America
ISBN 0-89283-196-0

 2  3  4  5  6  7  8  9  10  89  88  87  86  85  84

# Contents

# Introduction

OUR PRIVILEGED DUTY IN LIFE is to praise and glorify God as sovereign Lord of heaven and earth. Our whole life must be dedicated to this end. As we behold the Lord in all his majesty and splendor, our natural response is to praise him.

One of the time-honored methods of praising God as Creator and King, as Provider and Protector, is by praying those inspired hymns of praise which make up the Psalter.

The psalms are prayers that help us express the praise arising in our hearts. They are also expressions of adoration, worship, and honor to our glorious Lord and God. Through the words of the psalms we can voice gratitude to our loving and provident Father. The psalms give us the assurance of God's forgiving, healing love. They tells us that "a humbled, contrite heart he will not spurn."

During our earthly sojourn our needs are many and varied. In the psalms we find prayers of petition which will fit all our needs. With the psalmist, we come to our gracious Father, bringing our loneliness, insecurity, lack of trust, and our need to be loved. We come to the Rock for strength and protection, for enlightenment and guidance. In short, we come to him in all our needs both physical and spiritual.

## Praise Leads to Knowledge

The psalms are the songs of people who knew God as a personal God. They experienced God. They knew him with their heart.

If we are to pray more fervently and enter into a deeper union with God, then we must know him as the Lord to whom we are speaking. We must relate to him as a personal God. God reveals much about himself in the psalms.

We cannot love a person we do not know, and we cannot know a person to whom we have not listened. Praising God in the words of the psalms, and listening to what he is saying to us, will help us know him better. Knowing him better will increase our love for him. Loving him more will bring us greater happiness.

## Salvation History

The psalms are a record of salvation history. They are historical as they relate God's dealing with his people in the Old Testament times. The psalms are also christological. They are full of the Incarnate Word. Jesus prayed the psalms. He confirmed the theology of the psalms by quoting them in his own teaching ministry. And certainly the psalms have an ecclesial dimension. They are used extensively in the liturgy of the church.

Even though the psalms were composed in the Old Testament, they are deeply trinitarian. To the Father is attributed the work of creation. His ongoing providential care is praised and glorified in many of the psalms. The royal psalms foretell the coming of the Messianic King. In the songs of Israel, God's work of sanctification performed by the Holy Spirit is praised and glorified.

The psalms present a summary of salvation history prior to the Incarnation. If we did not have any of the books of the Old Testament, we would still know much about God's revelation of himself and his dealing with his people. The psalms tell of his nature and praise him for his wonderful work.

## For Our Times

This accent on praying with the psalms is by no means new in the church. The psalms are the source of many different methods of prayer recommended by the church throughout the centuries. They play an important role in the sacramental liturgies of the church, especially in

4 / The Lord Is My Shepherd

the Eucharist. They also form the main body of the church's daily prayer—the Liturgy of the Hours.

We are also encouraged to pray the psalms privately. They are an ideal form of vocal prayer. Singing or reciting the psalms can also be an excellent method of communal prayer. Since the Psalter is the only divinely inspired book of prayer, it is particularly valuable for meditation.

In a variety of ways, the psalms can lead us into a greater depth of prayer. As we pray these hymns of praise, we are led more naturally into a contemplative posture.

The psalms are songs of praise, thanksgiving, joy, and petition, uttered by people who knew God as a personal God. They experienced God in their daily lives and attempted to express that personal experience in the psalms.

The Israelites recognized God's power, majesty, and transcendence living in the "heavens above the heavens." They knew him with their heart. They met him at the core of their being.

While they had a rich experience of God, the Israelites could not find the words to express this experience. Nor can we find words to verbalize our own awareness of God in our lives. No words have ever been coined that can convey such a contemplative experience. The psalmist struggled with this difficulty. He spoke of the mighty mountains, the power of the turbulent sea, the stability of a rock, the frightful flash of lightning, and the provider of the rain and sunshine for an abundant harvest. All these were feeble attempts to convey some impression of the psalmist's own experience of the transcendent God of heaven and earth.

This fact makes the psalms particularly relevant to our age. Today we are not overly preoccupied with rational or theological proofs for the existence of God. But we desperately desire to experience God. We long to know him with our heart rather than our intellect. We desire to experience his presence, his power, his love. Such experiences help us form a personal relationship with him.

The psalms are indeed meant for our age because they lead us gently, but profoundly, into contemplation. They are the windows through which we gaze to catch contemplative glimpses of God. They are the avenues which bring us into his presence and leave us to rest in the sunshine of his love.

## *Fruits*

One fundamental truth which the psalms can teach us is that real peace comes primarily from our submission to God's will and from our total trust and confidence in him as our loving Father. As we pray the psalms, we expose our thinking to God's word. There we discover his will. As we rest in his presence, our will becomes gradually conformed to his. This submission and this confidence in him are the source of great joy in our lives.

Many of the psalms are particularly appropriate for times of suffering and trial. At sometime or other, all of us have been wounded, scarred, or broken by the sinfulness of our human nature. Our relationships with others are often hampered by misunderstandings, conflicts, and injustice. One of the great evils in our times is man's inhumanity to man. As we contemplate the message of the psalms, we will find hope and reassurance, comfort and consolation. Without the psalms we might have gone our own way into despair.

Other psalms can help us when we are plunged into spiritual trial. There is no dryness, discouragement, or dark night of the soul which the psalmist has not experienced. The psalms show us how the suffering of the psalmist's time prefigured the agony of Jesus in the garden, his rejection and his death, which led eventually to his glorification. Thus, they bring us hope in our hour of suffering and lead us into joyful acceptance.

The most joyful and the most admirable of all the psalms are those that express praise and adoration of God. The real purpose of a psalm is to praise and glorify God. When we submit to God's will because he is so good to us, when we want to serve him because he is so loving, then joy overflows in our hearts. It is then that our hearts want to burst out with songs of praise. In fact the greatest joy we can experience comes from praising and glorifying God. As we enter into the spirit of praise which the psalms hold in store for us, then the Lord becomes the source of our joy. He is our inspiration and our motivation, our light and our strength.

The most moving of all the psalms are those messianic songs in which the soul vividly perceives the suffering and triumph of Christ as our glorified Savior. These great eschatological psalms keep our eyes riveted on our destiny and fill our hearts with sober and expectant joy as we contemplate the Second Coming of Jesus.

## *Format*

A consistent format is followed in the presentation of these thirty-one psalms in the following pages. The presentation of each psalm is divided into five sections as a guideline for prayerful reflection.

1. Introduction
2. The Psalm
3. Reflections
4. The Life of Jesus
5. The Life of the Church

**Introduction.** A brief introduction offers a glimpse into the theme of the psalm, or some hint about its relevance or its meaning for us today.

**The Psalm.** The text of the psalm is the inspired word of God. He speaks to us personally and individually as we ponder his word, listening at the very depth of our being. The text merits our prolonged pondering.

**Reflections.** The reflection or commentary may give a brief explanation of a word, phrase, or thought, designed to guide us into a prayerful mood.

**The Life of Jesus.** Just how did Jesus use the psalms? How did he use them for prayer, for teaching? This section highlights the christological dimensions of the psalms. It is worth noting that 110 of 150 psalms which make up the Psalter are quoted or referred to in the New Testament.

**The Life of the Church.** How has the church incorporated the theme and meaning or even the text of a psalm in the liturgy or in church teaching? This section focuses on the ecclesial dimensions.

## How to Use This Book

One of the best ways to learn to appreciate the psalms is to acquire the habit of praying them slowly, reflectively, and consistently. The psalms are such a storehouse of inspiration that they can lead us into any form of prayer—vocal prayers, meditation, or contemplation.

The pages that follow include psalms as a source of prayer for each day of the month. The Lord may lead us to pray a certain psalm for several days. Because prayer is a gift from God, we must remain receptive to the kind of prayer in which he is leading us. We may feel drawn to use a psalm as vocal prayer, or as a source for meditation, or as a window through which we contemplatively behold God.

You may decide to randomly choose the psalm that you want to reflect on, but they do follow a specific plan in the text itself. The first group (Psalms 95, 131, 42) were selected to set the stage, to help us enter into prayer.

In the next sections, we praise God for his creative, provident, and merciful love. As we recall the boundless blessings which the Lord showers upon us each day, our appreciative hearts want to sing out in joy and thanksgiving. The psalms help us express deep sentiments of gratitude.

What better way is there to voice our prayers of petition before the Lord than to use the inspired words of the psalms? They help us plead for every need we have on our journey to our heavenly Father. Ultimately, they lead us into the perfect prayer of praise. In praising God, we adore and worship him; we extol and glorify him for himself. This is our primary duty in life.

If this small book takes us one step further in praising the Lord of heaven and earth, it has achieved its purpose. May God grace it to accomplish this end.

Borrowing the words of the psalmist, all the thoughts contained in this book can be summarized in his brief but beautiful hymn of praise.

> O praise the Lord, all you nations,
> acclaim him, all you peoples!
> Strong is his love for us;
> he is faithful for ever. (Ps 117)

# ONE

# Teach Us to Pray

## Psalm 95
### Call to Prayer

TO PROPERLY UNDERSTAND the psalms, we must realize that the psalms were the Israelites' attempts at expressing their experience of God. A bolt of lightning, the grandeur of a mountain, the warming sun, and the nourishing rain all reminded them of the abiding presence of the Lord. The psalms represent an effort to put into words their contemplative experience of God.

The psalmist sets forth two convincing reasons why the Israelites should praise and worship their God. First, as Creator and King, God deserves the worship of all his creatures. Second, as a providing, protecting Shepherd of the flock, he merits the trust and the gratitude of his chosen ones.

Psalm 95 invites us to celebrate God's goodness as our Creator and Lord. Furthermore, pondering his power and might should move us to a deep spirit of reverence and adoration.

In his goodness God chose us as his very own people. This is sufficient reason to make our hearts sing with joy.

Reflectively and joyfully let us pray:

*Come, let us sing to the Lord*
*and shout with joy to the rock who saves us.*
*Let us approach him with praise and thanksgiving*
*and sing joyful songs to the Lord.*

*The Lord is God, the mighty God,*
*the great king over all the gods.*
*He holds in his hands the depths of the earth*
*and the highest mountains as well.*
*He made the sea; it belongs to him,*
*the dry land, too, for it was formed by his hands.*

*Come, then, let us bow down and worship,*
*bending the knee before the Lord, our maker.*
*For he is our God and we are his people,*
*the flock he shepherds.*
*Today, listen to the voice of the Lord:*
*Do not grow stubborn, as your fathers did*
*in the wilderness,*
*when at Meriba and Massah*
*they challenged me and provoked me,*
*Although they had seen all of my works.*

*Forty years I endured that generation.*
*I said, "They are a people whose hearts go astray*
*and they do not know my ways."*

*So I swore in my anger,*
   *"They shall not enter into my rest."*

**Reflections.** The author makes several suggestions which will help us form proper attitudes for prayer. Reflecting on the goodness of the Lord should cause our hearts to "sing to the Lord and shout with joy." "The Lord is God, the mighty God, the great King" will inspire awe, reverence, and worship in his creatures.

The author also suggests a prayerful posture. "Let us bow down and worship, / bending the knee before the Lord, our maker." This posture helps us create within ourselves the spirit of humble worship.

The psalmist touches upon the key to a deep prayer experience when he urges, "Today, listen to the voice of the Lord." Attentive listening is praying. Listening is loving. We cannot love a person we do not know, and we cannot know a person unless we have listened to that person. The same axiom applies to our relationship with our loving Father.

The author cautions his people about an attitude which can ruin all efforts to pray. "Do not grow stubborn," challenging and provoking God. The ideal disposition for prayer is to approach the Lord humbly, open and receptive to his will.

Finally, the inspired writer warns what will

happen to "those people whose hearts go astray" saying, "They shall not enter into my rest."

While the psalmist uses the word "rest" to mean the Promised Land, we may rightly think of it as our eternal rest with the Lord in heaven.

**The Life of Jesus.** Jesus not only calls us to prayer, but he himself showed us by his own example the importance of taking time for prayer. He also taught us the essential dispositions for prayer.

A follower of Jesus must be prayerful in order to be a person of great joy. In revealing the Good News, Jesus told us about the loving concern of the Father for every detail of our life. The Father's concern is our source of genuine joy. "All this I tell you / that my joy may be yours / and your joy may be complete" (Jn 15:11).

Disciples of Jesus must radiate and reflect real joy regardless of the situations in which they may find themselves. Jesus advises us to be joyous even in suffering and persecution: "Blest are you when they insult you and persecute you and utter every kind of slander against you because of me. Be glad and rejoice, for your reward is great in heaven" (Mt 5:11).

Jesus takes up the refrain of the psalmist who says, "Listen to the voice of the Lord." Repeatedly Jesus underscored the necessity of coming to prayer with a listening heart.

In the parable of the sower we have a pastoral image of the seed falling upon four different kinds of seedbeds. In this graphic way Jesus taught us how essential an open, receptive, listening heart is to receiving the word of the Lord: "The seed on good ground are those who hear the word in a spirit of openness, retain it, and bear fruit through perseverance" (Lk 8:4ff).

The Father spoke forcefully at Jesus' Transfiguration: "This is my beloved Son on whom my favor rests. Listen to him" (Mt 17:5).

Jesus reiterated and explained more vividly the psalmist's warning about the proper dispositions for prayer. The people challenged and provoked God. And Jesus said, "If you bring your gift to the altar and there you recall that your brother has anything against you, leave your gift at the altar, go first to be reconciled with your brother, and then come and offer your gift" (Mt 5:23f).

On other occasions Jesus encouraged us to pray, not like "the learned and the clever," but with the heart of a child.

**The Life of the Church.** Prayer *is* our relationship with our loving Father. When we ponder his might and power, his love and compassion, his mercy and forgiveness, then we are praying.

To help us foster the proper dispositions for prayer, the church calls us to praise and worship God by beginning the Liturgy of the Hours every day with this special psalm—Psalm 95. The church has incorporated all the directives of Psalm 95 in the Mass. In every Mass we celebrate with joy, as we worship our "mighty God, the great king," and we "bow down and worship, / bending the knee before the Lord, our maker."

## Psalm 131
### Disposition for Prayer

The proper attitudes for prayer are briefly but clearly outlined in Psalm 131. In spite of the psalm's brevity, the psalmist guides us into an ideal posture for prayer.

This psalm perfectly expresses the childlike confidence and trust which should characterize all who are the privileged, adopted daughters and sons of our loving Father. Our loving trust is the source of great peace and joy—the fruit of our willingness to accept whatever God is asking of us.

As we come to prayer, our attitude must be the same as that of children seeking to be loved and striving to love in turn.

*O Lord, my heart is not proud*
*nor haughty my eyes.*
*I have not gone after things too great*
*nor marvels beyond me.*

*Truly I have set my soul*
*in silence and peace.*

*As a child has rest in its mother's arms,*
*even so my soul.*

*O Israel, hope in the Lord*
*both now and for ever.*

**Reflections.** "O Lord, my heart is not proud / nor haughty my eyes." As we address these words to God, it is not our intention to remind God that our heart is not haughty nor arrogant. Rather, the words remind us that we must come to prayer with great humility, acknowledging our total dependence upon God. "I have not gone after things too great / nor marvels beyond me."

If we want to pray well, we must first recognize that prayer is a gift from God. On our part, we must give God the gift of our time and attention, coming to him with humble trust and confidence. Worldly ambitions are obstacles to a deep union with God in prayer. Unwittingly, in our daily round of duties, we can become engrossed in programs, plans, and projects which leave little or no time for God. Even if we do want to pray, our minds are often cluttered with mundane preoccupations, making prayer very difficult. "Truly I have set my soul in silence and peace / As a child has rest in its mother's arms." This beautiful image of a child resting "in its mother's arms" speaks volumes to us about our own prayer-posture, resting in the arms of our loving Father. A child rests in its mother's arms only to bask in the reassuring comfort and warmth of its mother's love. Furthermore, the trust and love of this child brings joy to the mother's heart. Our resting and relaxing in our loving Father's presence brings him much joy.

Our presence with the Lord in prayer is our response in love to our caring Father. Even though nothing may seem to be "happening" in our prayer, our very presence is a prayerful response to our loving Lord.

"O Israel, hope in the Lord / both now and for ever." We are the new Israel. The psalmist issues an urgent appeal to all of us to place our hope and trust in the Lord.

**The Life of Jesus.** Jesus had a special love for the lowly. The Father will not reveal himself to the proud and haughty. Jesus rejoiced that the Father made himself known to the little people. "Father, Lord of heaven and earth, to you I offer praise; for what you have hidden from the learned and clever you have revealed to the merest children. Father it is true. You have graciously willed it so" (Mt 11:25ff).

In order to develop this humble attitude in prayer, Jesus says, "Learn from me, for I am gentle and humble of heart" (Mt 11:29). Jesus even made having this attitude a condition for entering heaven. "I assure you, unless you change and become like little children, you will not enter the kingdom of God" (Mt 18:1ff).

**The Life of the Church.** Jesus tells us that he did not go "after things too great." Every time the people wanted to make him a king, he escaped and went off to pray. "The Son of Man has come, not to be served by others, but to serve, to give his own life as a ransom for the many" (Mt 20:28).

Jesus tells us that he was single-hearted in doing the Father's will at all times. He also warns us against the possibility of trying to serve two masters: "No man can serve two masters. He will either hate the one and love the other or be attentive to one and despise the other. You cannot give yourself to God and money" (Mt 6:24).

Jesus set "his soul in silence and peace." Repeatedly he went off to a desert area, or a mountaintop to seek solitude in prayer. "Rising early the next morning, he went off to a lonely place in the desert, there he was absorbed in prayer" (Mk 1:25). And again, "He went out to the mountain to pray, spending the night in communion with God" (Lk 6:12).

Jesus really lived the spirit of this psalm. He encourages us to put our "hope in the Lord, both now and for ever." "Do not let your hearts be troubled. Have faith in God and faith in me" (Jn 14:1).

Let us beg Jesus to be with us as we pray Psalm

131 so that we may enter into a rich, prayerful experience humbly, serenely, trustingly, as a child resting in its father's arms.

## Psalm 42
### Ardent Yearning

Within every human being is a restlessness, a searching for something beyond ourselves. This desire is a longing for God and for a better knowledge of him as a personal God. This restlessness can be mitigated and can even reach a degree of fulfillment through prayer.

Prayer is a seeking, a longing to experience God. It is a desire to form a more personal relationship with our loving Father, with Jesus our risen Lord, and with the Holy Spirit dwelling within us and making us his Temple.

This desire can become so intense that it is rightly called a hunger and a thirst for God. A longing to know God better, to establish a love-relationship with him, is already prayer.

Many of the psalms attempt to verbalize the psalmists' experience of God. By this verbalization the psalmists try to keep alive in themselves and in others an experiential awareness of God.

In Psalm 42, the author prays fervently to become more aware of God's presence within him. He experiences an emptiness within his own soul, and he cries out from the depth of his being for an awareness of God's loving presence.

The psalmist is probably an exile from Jerusalem, the holy city. He yearns for the happiness he once enjoyed celebrating the great feasts in the Temple, where he experienced the presence of God.

Like the psalmist, we are exiles in this land of sojourn. We, too, are aware of a loneliness, an emptiness, an unfulfilled yearning within ourselves. Such feelings can lead us into prayer.

As we pray this psalm, we become more conscious of our own exile. This awareness creates a deeper longing, a stronger desire, a more ardent yearning for a richer, more personal relationship with God. Together with the psalmist, let us pray.

> *Like the deer that yearns*
> *for running streams,*
> *so my soul is yearning*
> *for you, my God.*
>
> *My soul is thirsting for God,*
> *the God of my life;*
> *when can I enter and see*
> *the face of God?*
>
> *My tears have become my bread,*
> *by night, by day,*
> *as I hear it said all the day long:*
> *"Where is your God?"*

These things will I remember
as I pour out my soul:
how I would lead the rejoicing crowd
into the house of God,
amid cries of gladness and thanksgiving,
the throng wild with joy.

Why are you cast down, my soul,
why groan within me?
Hope in God; I will praise him still,
my saviour and my God.

My soul is cast down within me
as I think of you,
from the country of Jordan and Mount Hermon,
from the Hill of Mizar.

Deep is calling on deep,
in the roar of waters;
your torrents and all your waves
swept over me.

By day the Lord will send
his loving kindness;
by night I will sing to him,
praise the God of my life.

I will say to God, my rock:
"Why have you forgotten me?
Why do I go mourning
oppressed by the foe?"

With cries that pierce me to the heart,
my enemies revile me,

*saying to me all the day long:*
*"Where is your God?"*

*Why are you cast down, my soul,*
*why groan within me?*
*Hope in God; I will praise him still,*
*my saviour and my God.*

**Reflections.** "Like the deer that yearns for running streams" is a beautiful pastoral image. We can readily picture a deer searching for fresh water with eyes scanning the landscape, nostrils extended to catch a scent, and ears poised listening for the sound of "running streams." Like the deer, we use all our external senses to catch a glimpse of God.

"My soul is yearning for you, my God" expresses the psalmist's longing for an internal experience of God. We, too, long to experience his presence through the love, peace, and joy with which he blesses us by his presence.

"Deep is calling on deep" is a reminder to the psalmist that he is in exile. At the headwaters of the Jordan River, pouring forth from the base of Mt. Hermon, is a magnificent waterfall. Many cataracts interrupt its even flow southward. The roar of the water made the psalmist think of the reverberations of the hymns of praise resounding in the Temple.

The entire poem is an unselfish expression of yearning for God with no expectation of reward.

"With cries that pierce me to the heart, my enemies revile me." In spite of the taunts and derision of his enemies, the psalmist never loses hope, but continues to praise God.

Hope in God; I will praise him still,
my saviour and my God.

**The Life of Jesus.** Jesus knew that God-given desires would well up within us. He shows us that the only way this longing can be fulfilled is through him. "I am the way, and the truth, and the life; / No one comes to the Father but through me." (Jn 14:6)

Jesus promised that he could fulfill this desire within us. "I myself am the bread of life. / No one who comes to me shall ever be hungry / no one who believes in me shall ever thirst." (Jn 6:35)

The gift of himself in the Holy Eucharist, then, will satisfy our desire for him. When he blesses us with an experiential awareness of his presence in us, we shall find great fulfillment.

Next Jesus invites us to come to him. "If anyone thirsts, let him come to me; / Let him drink who believes in me. / From within him rivers of living water shall flow" (Jn 7:37f).

As Jesus fills us with this divine life and love, we will be able to radiate his love, peace, and joy to others. These are the rivers of living water.

**The Life of the Church.** As we meet the Lord every day in our prayer time, our personal relationship with him will grow and mature. He alone can satisfy our longing and yearning. When we come to know him better, he then calls us friends (Jn 15:14f).

The psalmist longs for Mount Zion and the Temple. Ours is a much greater privilege. Our destiny is to form a deep love-relationship enabling us to "see the face of God." We shall encounter him not only in our contemplative prayer, but one day "we shall see him as he is" (1 Jn 3:2). Then we shall be able to radiate and reflect his presence in us to others. He will channel his divine life and love through us. "For God who said, 'Let light shine out of darkness,' has shone in our hearts that we in turn might make known the glory of God shining on the face of Christ" (2 Cor 4:6).

What wonder, what majesty, what grandeur, what joy awaits us!

# Way of Life

### Psalm 1
### Two Standards

IN THE *SPIRITUAL EXERCISES,* St. Ignatius leads us into a meditation on two standards: the standard of Lucifer, and the standard of Jesus. Lucifer strives to lure us away from the Lord by the enticement of riches, position, and pride. The standard of Jesus is diametrically opposed to that of Lucifer. Jesus tells us that if we follow his standard we must be poor, willing to be looked down upon or laughed at, and like him we must be humble. In Psalm 1, the writer holds up to us two standards. The way of the Lord brings happiness, while the way of the wicked ends like chaff to be discarded and burned.

For St. Ignatius and the psalmist it is either black or white. Neither one admits a grey area between these two standards. Surely both of these gifted writers were well aware that, given our human nature, there is a mixture of both good and bad within us. With St. Paul we can certainly say: "What happens is that I do, not the good I will to do, but the evil I do not intend" (Rom 7:18f).

Aware of our brokenness, we know that we will never fully reach either extreme of virtue or vice. God looks only at our intention and our striving. If our fundamental option is to serve him faithfully by choosing his standard, then he is pleased with us even if we do not achieve the goal we have set for ourselves.

> *Happy indeed is the man*
> *who follows not the counsel of the wicked;*
> *nor lingers in the way of sinners*
> *nor sits in the company of scorners,*
> *but whose delight is the law of the Lord*
> *and who ponders his law day and night.*
>
> *He is like a tree that is planted*
> *beside the flowing waters,*
> *that yields its fruit in due season*
> *and whose leaves shall never fade;*
> *and all that he does shall prosper.*
> *Not so are the wicked, not so!*
>
> *For they like winnowed chaff*
> *shall be driven away by the wind.*
> *When the wicked are judged they shall not stand,*
> *nor find room among those who are just;*
> *for the Lord guards the way of the just*
> *but the way of the wicked leads to doom.*

**Reflections.** In his opening words the psalmist reminds us that our fall is usually a gradual one. It may even begin without us being aware of it. We may slip from one stage into the second and third. We may first follow the counsel of the wicked, next linger, and finally sit with them. The psalmist cautions us about these three steps. "Happy indeed is the man / *who follows not* the counsel of the wicked; / *nor lingers* in the way of sinners / *nor sits* in the company of scorners." (emphasis added)

The psalmist reveals a deep insight into man's humanness scarred by sin. He also stresses the joy that results from avoiding evil and from pursuing the Lord.

The good person is portrayed "like a tree that is planted beside the flowing waters." The Hebrews often thought in images. To describe the just person as a fruitful tree is not uncommon. Jesus used a similar illustration: "A good tree does not produce decayed fruit any more than a decayed tree produces good fruit. Each tree is known by its yield" (Lk 6:43).

In sharp contrast to the good person is the wicked person who is called "chaff" by the author. This is a telling illustration. In the psalmist's day the winnowing process was used to thresh out the wheat. The threshing floor was usually a breezy mound where the wind played an important role in the winnowing procedure. The grain was stamped out either by a person or by an animal treading over the stocks of wheat. After this, the straw was shaken into the wind, with the chaff being blown away and the grains of wheat remaining on the threshing floor. Like the discarded chaff, so the wicked are blown away. "The way of the wicked leads to doom."

**The Life of Jesus.** In proclaiming the Good News, Jesus set forth two standards: "He who is not with me is against me, / and he who does not gather with me scatters" (Lk 11:23).

At another time Jesus reiterated how important it is for us to keep our focus on him. "No man can serve two masters. He will either hate one and love the other or be attentive to one and despise the other. You cannot give yourself to God and money" (Mt 6:24).

The teaching of Jesus, however, is never purely negative. He always suggests a positive mode of action. How briefly, but yet how clearly he set forth the path we are to follow: "I am the way, and the truth, and the life" (Jn 14:6).

Jesus showed us the way when he gave us the Beatitudes in the Sermon on the Mount. These Beatitudes are really eight ways to follow Jesus and imitate his way of life. In effect, he is telling us that he is poor in spirit. We will be blessed if we, like him, are poor in spirit. Thus he outlined eight different pathways by which we can follow him and be recognized as his disciples.

**The Life of the Church.** Jesus calls each one of us to follow him closely so that we might become like him. St. Paul urges, "Put on that new man created in God's image" (Eph 4:23). Following Jesus requires a constant commitment and recommitment to his way of life. Daily we face new challenges, different duties, and various approaches in responding to the needs of the people God sends across our path. Our life must be one of ongoing conversion. The conversion may not involve a drastic change, but a constant and consistent turning to God. The multiplicity of daily demands, duties, and distractions often deflects us from our direct course.

Our daily date with the Lord in prayer helps us to discern and to discover those influences which may wean us away from our total commitment to him. A continual refocusing and rededication is necessary to keep us under his banner.

How well we accomplish this rededication depends upon how much we love. As our love for Jesus matures, we will be more and more drawn to his standard while the standard of the evil one becomes less and less enticing.

Happy indeed will we be!

### Psalm 5
### Morning Prayer

Someone put it well when they said, "A task

well-begun is already half finished." This truism can be readily applied to the beginning of a new day. If we begin our day with the Lord, we will be better able to accept the happenings of the day with enthusiasm, peace, and joy. For this reason, spiritual writers have highly recommended the morning hours as an ideal time for prayer.

The psalmist prayerfully begins his day in order to meet anything and anyone who would threaten or shake his trust in God. Fortunately he recognizes every trial and test as a means to bring him into a greater dependence upon God.

Each day, we, too, face difficulties from without as well as problems from within. The trials of each day will keep us aware of our own inadequacy to cope with them and our need for an ever-increasing confidence and trust in the Lord.

In our daily morning prayer, we may wish to include the prayer of the psalmist.

*To my words give ear, O Lord,*
*give heed to my groaning.*
*Attend to the sound of my cries,*
*my King and my God.*

*It is you whom I invoke, O Lord.*
*In the morning you hear me;*
*in the morning I offer you my prayer,*
*watching and waiting.*

*You are no God who loves evil;*
*no sinner is your guest.*

*The boastful shall not stand their ground*
*before your face.*

*You hate all who do evil:*
*you destroy all who lie.*
*The deceitful and bloodthirsty man*
*the Lord detests.*

*But I through the greatness of your love*
*have access to your house.*
*I bow down before your holy temple,*
*filled with awe.*

*Lead me, Lord, in your justice,*
*because of those who lie in wait;*
*make clear your way before me.*

*No truth can be found in their mouths,*
*their heart is all mischief,*
*their throat a wide-open grave,*
*all honey their speech.*

*All those you protect shall be glad*
*and ring out their joy.*
*You shelter them, in you they rejoice,*
*those who love your name.*

*It is you who bless the just man, Lord:*
*you surround him with favor as with a shield.*

**Reflections.** The psalmist begins with an earnest
appeal begging the Lord, "attend to the sound of
my cries, my King and my God." Notice that he
recognizes his relationship to God. He calls him

"King and God" to acknowledge his own relationship as a creature addressing the supreme Lord of heaven and earth.

"In the morning I offer my prayer, watching and waiting" is an expression of the new hope and expectation with which the psalmist begins each day. There is a newness, a stillness, a thankfulness, an energy about the morning which engenders enthusiasm and expectation. By the mercy and goodness of God we, too, begin the day with great hope of better things to come.

"You are no God who loves evil." In these words the psalmist reminds himself that the nature of God is diametrically opposed to the nature of sin. The psalmist finds courage and hope for the new day realizing that God will protect him and give him the strength to deal with his enemies. Even more, God himself will not permit them to harm him.

The Holy Spirit reminded St. Paul of the same truth when he sought help in adversity: "My grace is enough for you, for in weakness power reaches perfection" (2 Cor 12:9).

With a fitting conclusion to his morning prayer, the psalmist praises God for his protection. He, himself, is one who will ring out his joy and rejoice in the goodness of God, who shelters those who love him, who blesses and surrounds the just man with favor.

**The Life of Jesus.** It is not surprising that Jesus showed us the advantage of using the morning hours for prayer. After spending the whole evening healing and expelling demons, Jesus rose early the next morning to spend some time in prayer with the Father. "Rising early the next morning, he went off to a lonely place in the desert; there he was absorbed in prayer" (Mk 1:35).

**The Life of the Church.** Morning can be an the ideal time for prayer. Upon rising, we are more relaxed than during the hours of the day. Listening to the Lord is often easier. Another great advantage to spending time in morning prayer is that it focuses our attention on God, allowing him to form our attitude to the day ahead of us.

Prayer is the gift of our time and attention to our loving Father. It may be expressed in various ways. Our prayer may consist of a vocal offering of the day to the Lord as a special love-offering of self. We may pray a kind of prayer of abandonment to God's design for the day, as suggested by Brother Charles of Jesus. The words and formula are not of prime importance. The dispositions which they develop within us are more important. They mold and shape our attitudes toward the happenings of the day.

Our morning prayer may be a meditation or

reflection on the gift of life for a new day, or the manifold blessings which have already been showered upon us, or a reflection on some words of scripture to give us a sense of direction.

We may wish to take a contemplative approach to our morning prayer. Using this method we simply make a gift of ourselves to God, basking in his presence, permitting him to love us and in this fashion transform our hearts.

Morning prayer will brighten our day, cheer our hearts, help us to smile more easily, and enable us to radiate the Lord's love, peace, and joy.

## Psalm 4
### Evening Prayer

Each day as the sunset hours approach and we rest from the labors of the day, we enter more deeply into a state of relaxation. This time can be especially conducive to prayer.

As we recall the blessings of the day, sentiments of joy and gratitude begin to well up in our hearts. As our reflection on God's goodness throughout the day continues, we may become painfully aware of our shortcomings and our neglect of duty. Our prayer becomes not only one of thanksgiving, but one of sorrow as well. We are naturally inclined to ask for forgiveness for the faults and failings of the day. For these reasons, the evening hours of the day have led

Christians into a prayerful attitude.

Evening prayer is not new to our age nor peculiar to our Christian era. The tradition of evening prayer has come down to us from ages long past. The people of old found this time of day a natural time for prayer. In the Psalter are found many prayers of praise, thanksgiving, and sorrow which have been appropriately used for prayer as the evening shadows envelop the world.

Psalm 4 is an ideal prayer of thanksgiving as the twilight hours remind us that night is fast approaching. With the psalmist, let us devoutly give thanks.

*When I call, answer me, O God of justice;*
*from anguish you released me; have mercy and hear*
*   me!*

*O men, how long will your hearts be closed,*
*will you love what is futile and seek what is false?*

*It is the Lord who grants favors to those whom he*
*   loves;*
*the Lord hears me whenever I call him.*

*Fear him; do not sin; ponder on your bed and be*
*   still.*
*Make justice your sacrifice and trust in the Lord.*

*"What can bring us happiness?" many say.*
*Let the light of your face shine on us, O Lord.*

*You have put into my heart a greater joy
than they have from abundance of corn and new
wine.*

*I will lie down in peace and sleep comes at once
for you alone, Lord, make me dwell in safety.*

## Reflections.

When I call, answer me, O God of justice;
from anguish you released me; have mercy and
hear me!

The psalmist makes it clear that to fail to
express our gratitude is blameworthy, but to
refuse to ask is a much greater offense. God wants
to be a generous and gracious Abba, but he also
wants us to ask for his gifts.

Asking clarifies our petition in our own minds
and keeps us aware of our dependence upon our
loving Father. How earnestly the psalmist begs
the Lord to hear him.

"Ponder on your bed and be still" is a clear
directive encouraging us into a proper disposition for prayer at the close of the day. As we
ponder the Lord's goodness, it will be easier to
"fear him; do not sin."

"Make justice your sacrifice and trust in the
Lord" is an eloquent way of telling us to bring the
gift of ourselves to the Lord and be confident that

he will be pleased with the efforts of the day.

Trusting in the Lord and doing his will can bring us more happiness than an abundance of material gifts. In a few well-chosen words the psalmist expresses this truism: "You have put into my heart a greater joy / than they have from abundance of corn and new wine."

The abundance of corn and new wine refers to the harvest celebrations. The psalmist assures his hearers that to enjoy the harvest and all the other temporal gifts of the Lord is proper and praiseworthy. These gifts should give us much joy. However, the happiness and peace which he experiences is much more satisfying and lasting, because he simply seeks God, himself, and a deeper union with him. He seeks the giver rather than the gifts. His own words express it more accurately: "I will lie down in peace and sleep comes at once / for you alone, Lord, make me dwell in safety."

When we are at peace with the Lord, then we will be at peace with ourselves and with our brothers and sisters.

**The Life of Jesus.** Jesus, himself, found the evening hours suitable for prayer. At night, after long days of teaching, healing, and preaching, he often retired to the desert or to a mountaintop to be alone with his Father. "Then he went out to the mountain to pray, / spending the night in communion with God" (Lk 6:12). On another occasion after feeding the multitude, he dismissed his disciples and went out by himself to pray. "When he had sent them away, he went up on the mountain by himself to pray, remaining there alone as evening drew on" (Mt 14:23f).

During the closing days of his life, Jesus spent the day teaching and talking with his enemies in the Temple area. When evening came, he went to the Mount of Olives to rest and pray.

Jesus' use of the evening hours as a time of prayer speaks eloquently to us of the appropriateness of this time of day for prayer.

**The Life of the Church.** From the earliest years, I am sure that all of us were taught the importance of evening prayer. I recall my own mother trying to break me of the habit of dubbing them "my bed prayers."

In the Liturgy of the Hours, which the church encourages us to pray, we find the psalms of both Evening Prayer and Night Prayer replete with expressions of praise and thanksgiving to God for his bountiful goodness to us throughout the day.

Some of the psalms arranged for these Hours also remind us of our waywardness and our need for the forgiving, healing love of the Lord as night approaches (e.g., Psalm 130—Night Prayer for Wednesday).

# THREE

# Creative Love

### Psalm 104
### God the Creator

PSALM 104 IS A MAGNIFICENT hymn praising God as the Creator of everything. It is one of the most remarkable songs in the whole Psalter. In the book of Genesis, the work of creation is described in brief phrases. In this hymn, the author portrays God's works of creation in vivid, rhythmic colors.

As the psalmist ponders the whole of creation, he is deeply moved and approaches God in a spirit of awe and reverence, with joy and praise. With the psalmist, let us reverently contemplate the might and majesty of God as revealed in the marvels of his creation.

*Bless the Lord, my soul!*
*Lord God, how great you are,*
*clothed in majesty and glory,*
*wrapped in light as in a robe!*

You stretch out the heavens like a tent.
Above the rains you build your dwelling.
You make the clouds your chariot,
and walk on the wings of the wind;
you make the winds your messengers
and flashing fire your servants.

You founded the earth on its base,
to stand firm from age to age.
You wrapped it with the ocean like a cloak:
the waters stood higher than the mountains.

At your threat they took to flight;
at the voice of your thunder they fled.
They rose over the mountains and flowed down
to the place which you had appointed.
You set limits they might not pass
lest they return to cover the earth.

You make springs gush forth in the valleys:
they flow in between the hills.
They give drink to all the beasts of the field;
the wild-asses quench their thirst.
On their banks dwell the birds of heaven;
from the branches they sing their song.

From your dwelling you water the hills;
earth drinks its fill of your gift.
You made the grass grow for the cattle
and the plants to serve man's needs,

that he may bring forth bread from the earth
and wine to cheer man's heart;

*oil, to make him glad
and bread to strengthen man's heart.*

*The trees of the Lord drink their fill,
the cedars he planted on Lebanon;
there the birds build their nests:
on the treetop the stork has her home.
The goats find a home on the mountains
and rabbits hide in the rocks.*

*You made the moon to mark the months;
the sun knows the time for its setting.
When you spread the darkness it is night
and all the beasts of the forest creep forth.
The young lions roar for their prey
and ask their food from God.*

*At the rising of the sun they steal away
and go to rest in their dens.
Man goes forth to his work,
to labor till evening falls.*

*How many are your works, O Lord!
In wisdom you have made them all.
The earth is full of your riches.*

*There is the sea, vast and wide,
with its moving swarms past counting,
living things great and small.
The ships are moving there
and the monsters you made to play with.*

*All of these look to you
to give them their food in due season.*

*You give it, they gather it up:*
*you open your hand, they have their fill.*

*You hide your face, they are dismayed;*
*you take back your spirit, they die,*
*returning to the dust from which they came.*
*You send forth your spirit, they are created;*
*and you renew the face of the earth.*

*May the glory of the Lord last for ever!*
*May the Lord rejoice in his works!*
*He looks on the earth and it trembles;*
*the mountains send forth smoke at his touch.*

*I will sing to the Lord all my life,*
*make music to my God while I live.*
*May my thoughts be pleasing to him.*
*I find my joy in the Lord.*
*Let sinners vanish from the earth*
*and the wicked exist no more.*
*Bless the Lord, my soul.*

**Reflections.** The seven stages of creation are significant. To the Hebrew, seven is a sacred number. Seven also corresponds to the seven days of creation as recorded in Genesis.

*Stage 1:* "You stretched out the heavens like a tent."

The rich imagery of these first four verses depicts the heavenly dwelling place of the Lord and Master of creation.

*Stage 2:* "You wrapped it with the ocean like a cloak."

Like his contemporaries, the psalmist thought of the planet as being completely inundated with water. Only in the process of creation did God make the dry land appear. Poetically, he relates this action of the Creator.

*Stage 3:* "You make springs gush forth in the valleys."

Verses ten to nineteen give a picturesque portrayal of the Lord caring for the needs of the "beasts of the field . . . the birds of heaven" as well as "to serve man's needs."

Well irrigated by streams of life-giving water, the land produces food and drink for all creatures: plants, animals, birds, and man. Realizing God's plan, lifts the heart of the psalmist in praise and thanksgiving.

*Stage 4:* "You made the moon to mark the months. . . ."

From the rising to the setting of the sun, from twilight through darkness into dawn, God's creative, sustaining love is present and operative. Again the psalmist's description is unique, colorful, and enjoyable.

*Stage 5:* "How many are your works, O Lord!"

The mysteries of the "sea, vast and wide with its moving swarms past counting" is another segment of God's magnificent creation. God's infinite love is translated into the works of his creation.

*Stage 6:* "All of these look to you to give them their food in due season."

God's love extends far beyond creation. His love energizes, saturates, sustains, and provides for all his creation through the power of his Spirit.

*Stage 7:* "May the glory of the Lord last for ever!"

Excited about the might and power of God, the psalmist prays that all creatures will respond to God's love so that the Lord may rejoice in his works.

Amazed at the omnipotence of God so manifest in creation, the psalmist promises, "I will sing to the Lord all my life." Then he bursts forth, "Bless the Lord, my soul."

**The Life of Jesus.** The principal avenues by which we come to appreciate God's mighty work of creation are our external senses. Our gracious God created and endowed us with the gift of our senses so that we might be led to a greater awareness of his creative, caring love.

Jesus urges us to use our external senses that we may grow in our relationship with our heavenly Father.

*Sight:* "Look at the birds of the sky.... Learn a lesson from the way the wild flowers grow." (Mt 6:26, 28)

*Hearing:* As Jesus began the parable of the sower going out to sow his seed, he bade his audience, "Listen carefully to this" (Mk 4:3). And the Father, too, urgently advised, "Listen to him!" (Mt 17:5).

*Touch:* In almost all the cases of Jesus healing someone, he touched the person in need of healing. "Jesus stretched out his hand and touched him" (Mt 8:3).

Others were healed by simply touching him: "All who touched him got well" (Mk 6:56).

His touch was also a blessing: "People were bringing their little children to him to have him touch them" (Mk 10:13).

Faith also comes through sight and touch: "Look at my hands and my feet; it is really I. Touch me, and see that a ghost does not have flesh and bones as I do" (Lk 24:39).

*Taste:* "The waiter in charge tasted the water made wine. . . . What you have done is keep the choice wine until now" (Jn 2:9ff).

*Smell:* "Lord, it has been four days now; surely there will be a stench" (Jn 11:39). Our olfactory nerves can remind us of the transitory nature of our lives. In this instance we are being made more aware of the power of Jesus over life and death.

Even though we may dimly see God in the magnificent work of his creation, we are deeply aware that all creation is only a faint reflection of his majesty.

**The Life of the Church.** God created our bodies with an extraordinary facility for movement. Body language can also bring us into a prayer posture: raising our eyes to heaven, kneeling in adoration, prostrating in humility, raising our hands in prayer, and sitting contemplatively in the sunshine of God's presence.

God's creative power extends far beyond our material world to the realm of the spiritual. We cannot grasp the "world" of the angels and saints with our external senses, but we know it by faith. Part of that spirit world is dwelling within us, but someday we shall be totally immersed in that community of perfect love.

Quoting the prophet Isaiah, St. Paul finds no words in which to describe that portion of God's creation. He simply says, "Eye has not seen, ear has not heard, nor has it so much as dawned on man what God has prepared for those who love him" (1 Cor 2:9).

Another sacred writer makes an attempt to lead us into a vision of heaven when he describes the "new Jerusalem, the holy city."

This is God dwelling among men. He shall

dwell with them and they shall be his people and he shall be their God who is always with them. He shall wipe every tear from their eyes, and there shall be no more death or mourning, crying out or pain, for the former world has passed away (Rv 21:3f).

"Bless the Lord, my soul."

## Psalm 8
### *Creaturely Dignity*

This psalm is a hymn of praise to God as Creator, especially for creating man in his own image and likeness. The psalmist contrasts the infinite majesty of God with the finite nature of human beings. He extols God for endowing us with so great a dignity.

God gave us a share in his creative power and gave us dominion over "the fish of the sea, the birds of the air, and the cattle, and over the wild animals and all creatures that crawl on the ground" (Gn 1:26). In turn, God asks us to bring creation to a higher state of perfection.

Our true dignity lies in the fact that "God created man in his image, / in the divine image he created him; / male and female he created them" (Gn 1:27).

The psalmist praises God because he made us the masterpiece of his creation.

*How great is your name, O Lord our God,*
*through all the earth!*

*Your majesty is praised above the heavens;*
*on the lips of children and of babes*
*you have found praise to foil your enemy,*
*to silence the foe and the rebel.*

*When I see the heavens, the work of your hands,*
*the moon and the stars which you arranged,*
*what is man that you should keep him in mind,*
*mortal man that you care for him?*

*Yet you have made him little less than a god;*
*with glory and honor you crowned him,*
*gave him power over the works of your hand,*
*put all things under his feet.*

*All of them, sheep and cattle,*
*yes, even the savage beasts,*
*birds of the air, and fish*
*that make their way through the waters.*

*How great is your name, O Lord our God,*
*through all the earth!*

**Reflections.** The psalmist is thrilled at the majesty and goodness of God. His heart breaks forth with a hymn of praise. There is no limit to the praise which God's majesty deserves. He is praised above the heavens: "How great is your name, O Lord our God!"

Even though creation is only a slight reflection of God's beauty and power, the psalmist, contemplatively beholding the sun, moon, and stars, is moved to praise and extol the God of creation: "When I see the heavens, the work of your hands."

God endowed man with a mind capable of grasping, even though only dimly, the infinite magnitude of the God of all creation. He gave man a heart which extols and glorifies the Lord's incomprehensible greatness: "What is man that you should keep him in mind?"

Man towers over the moon and stars, over the "sheep and the cattle, yes, even over the savage beasts, birds of the air and fish that make their way through the water." God gave man power over all these works of his creation, and he is superior to all these because he has a mind and heart with which to praise God. Man is the masterpiece of God's creation, because he reflects more fully the divine glory of God: "You . . . gave him power over the works of your hand."

The psalmist is singing here of the first Adam. The second Adam is even greater.

**The Life of Jesus.** Jesus took on our human nature with all its limitations. Thus he endowed men and women with an even greater dignity. "Though he was in the form of God / he did not deem equality with God / something to be grasped at. / Rather, he emptied himself and / took on the form of a slave, / being born in the likeness of men" (Phil 2:6f).

Jesus took our broken human nature down to death with him, so that he could redeem us and make us capable of sharing in his divine life. "If we have been united with him through likeness to his death, so shall we be through a like resurrection" (Rom 6:3ff).

The real dignity of every Christian, then, arises from the indwelling of the risen Jesus. "Anyone who loves me / will be true to my word, / and my Father will love him; / we will come to him / and make our dwelling place with him" (Jn 14:23).

The psalmist admires the first Adam created by God. As Christians, we admire the second Adam, Jesus, who raised us to an incomprehensible dignity. "Jesus, who was made for a little while lower than the angels, that through God's gracious will he might taste death for the sake of all men" (Heb 2:9).

**The Life of the Church.** Through Baptism we become the temples of the Holy Spirit. This bestows on us a dignity far beyond that of all the other works of God's creation. "You must know that your body is a temple of the Holy Spirit, who is within—the Spirit you have received from God. You are not your own. You have been purchased, and at a price! So glorify God in your body" (1 Cor 6:19).

Explaining to us the necessity of reaching out in loving kindness to others, Jesus makes a strong point. "I assure you, as often as you did it for one of my least brothers, you did it for me" (Mt 25:40).

Jesus could never have made such a declaration if he were not dwelling within every Christian man, woman, and child. This realization caused Paul to exclaim, "The life I live now is not my own; Christ is living in me" (Gal 2:20).

Even a brief reflection on the unique dignity with which God endowed us, makes our hearts sing out with the psalmist. "How great is your name, O Lord our God, / through all the earth!"

## Psalm 148
### All Creation's Hymn of Praise

When the psalmist ponders the mighty works of God's creation, he is awed at the splendor and magnificence of God's power and love. Since all of this is beyond human comprehension, he bursts forth with a hymn of praise and calls upon the whole of creation to join him. He even appeals to the heavens above the heavens, which we cannot see, to unite its voice in praise of its Creator.

The focal point of his invitation is the people of God. The hymn begins in heaven, comes down to earth, and reaches its climax when all rational creatures lift their minds, hearts, and voices in praise of God.

We, too, are invited to praise the Lord. Let us accept that invitation.

*Praise the Lord from the heavens,*
*praise him in the heights.*
*Praise him, all his angels,*
*praise him, all his host.*

*Praise him, sun and moon,*
*praise him, shining stars.*
*Praise him, highest heavens*
*and the waters above the heavens.*

*Let them praise the name of the Lord.*
*He commanded: they were made.*
*He fixed them for ever,*
*gave a law which shall not pass away.*

*Praise the Lord from the earth,*
*sea creatures and all oceans,*
*fire and hail, snow and mist,*
*stormy winds that obey his word;*

*all mountains and hills,*
*all fruit trees and cedars,*
*beasts, wild and tame,*
*reptiles and birds on the wing;*

*all earth's kings and peoples,*
*earth's princes and rulers;*
*young men and maidens,*
*old men together with children.*

*Let them praise the name of the Lord*
*for he alone is exalted.*
*The splendor of his name*
*reaches beyond heaven and earth.*

*He exalts the strength of his people.*
*He is the praise of all his saints,*
*of the sons of Israel,*
*of the people to whom he comes close.*

**Reflections.** All the heavenly bodies are called upon to praise the Lord: "Praise the Lord from the heavens. . . ."

The writer calls upon the "highest heavens and the waters above the heavens." According to the scientific knowledge of that day, the rain was to come from the heavens above the heavens which we see. Again the mystery of God's creation is implied: "He commanded: they were made. / He fixed them for ever, / gave a law which shall not pass away."

The praise of God begins in the heavens, comes down to earth, and goes round the whole world. Finally the people of God are invited to join in. Notice that the whole hierarchy of human levels excludes no one: "Kings, princes, rulers, young men and maidens, old men and children."

Lightning, which the psalmist calls "fire," was a great mystery to the people of his day. Usually it was singled out from the rest of creation. In this instance it adds praise to the God who created it.

**The Life of Jesus.** Praise of God is a basic element in Christianity. In the New Testament praise is essentially the same as in the Old Testament. In the New Testament, praise is our response to Christ's gift manifest in his redemptive power.

At the advent of the Christian era, praise was much in evidence. When the angels announced the birth of Jesus, they praised God, "Glory to God in high heaven, peace on earth to those on whom his favor rests" (Lk 2:14).

After their visit to the holy family, the shepherds expressed their joy in praise of God. "The shepherds returned, glorifying and praising God for all they had heard and seen" (Lk 2:20).

Praise of God is one of the highlights in the New Testament. On one occasion, when Jesus healed the blind man on the road to Jericho, the man praised God. "At that very moment he was given his sight and began to follow him, giving God the glory. All the people witnessed it and they too gave praise to God" (Lk 18:43).

As Jesus made his triumphal entry into Jerusalem on Palm Sunday the people shouted "hosanna!" uttering a true hymn of praise.

**The Life of the Church.** The Church reminds us that we are the People of God. We are the beginning of the new creation, and through us the whole world is to be recreated, to the greater glory of God.

Praise and thanksgiving often go hand-in-hand in the liturgy. However, praise is directed more to the majesty of God, while thanksgiving focuses on the blessings which God has lavished upon us. Praise springs out of a heart filled with joy.

The often-repeated "Alleluia"—which means "praise Yahweh"—gives a lilt to liturgical prayer. Likewise, the "Glory to the Father. . ." in the Liturgy of the Hours expresses our joy as we praise the triune God.

In the Eucharistic Celebration, the "Glory to God in the Highest" manifests the joy of our hearts as we praise God for all his own attributes and for his gifts to us.

How appropriate it is for us to add our voices to that of the sacred writer who says, "To the One seated on the throne, / and to the Lamb / be praise and honor, glory and might, / forever and ever" (Rv 5:13).

# FOUR

# Caring Love

## Psalm 23
### Solicitous Shepherd

PSALM 23 IS PROBABLY THE BEST known and most widely used of the whole collection of inspired prayers. It portrays, in beautiful pastoral imagery, God as a Shepherd caring for his sheep.

The psalmist rejoices in God's provident care for him. His loving care as a Shepherd covers all contingencies: protection, guidance, nourishment, and above all, love.

God is also a host providing food and sustenance for the sheep he loves so dearly. He is a most gracious and generous host.

With an awareness of God's overwhelming love, let us pray with the psalmist.

*The Lord is my shepherd;*
*there is nothing I shall want.*
*Fresh and green are the pastures*

*where he gives me repose.*
*Near restful waters he leads me,*
*to revive my drooping spirit.*

*He guides me along the right path;*
*he is true to his name.*
*If I should walk in the valley of darkness*
*no evil would I fear.*
*You are there with your crook and your staff;*
*with these you give me comfort.*

*You have prepared a banquet for me*
*in the sight of my foes.*
*My head you have anointed with oil;*
*my cup is overflowing.*
*Surely goodness and kindness shall follow me*
*all the days of my life.*
*In the Lord's own house shall I dwell*
*forever and ever.*

**Reflections.** The psalmist realizes that God is the provider of everything he needs. He rejoices in that fact: "There is nothing I shall want."

As grazing land begins to dry up in the summer's heat, the shepherd must know where to find new grass. This picture manifests God's providential care: "Fresh and green are the pastures. . . ."

In order to find sufficient grazing during the hot summer, it is necessary to climb to higher ground. Often this means taking a path through a canyon where hostile animals may threaten the sheep. God, like a watchful shepherd, is ever on the alert to protect his sheep: "If I should walk in the valley of darkness, . . ."

The psalmist visualizes God as a host preparing a banquet to feed and nourish his sheep. A banquet speaks of a sumptuous meal, thanks to God's goodness and generosity: "You have prepared a banquet for me. . . ."

A perfumed oil was used at banquets to please the guests with its delicate aroma: "My head you have anointed with oil. . . ."

The psalmist hopes to live eternally with his shepherd in the bliss of heaven: "In the Lord's own house shall I dwell forever and ever."

**The Life of Jesus.** Jesus uses the same figure of speech in revealing his loving concern for every one of us. He says plainly, "I am the Good Shepherd" (Jn 10:11). Jesus invites us into the "green pastures" and "restful waters" of his divine presence. He invites us to spend time with him in prayer: to rest in his presence, to listen to the comforting, inspiring message of his word.

Jesus protects us with his crook and staff. As the shepherd's staff enables him to help a fully-coated sheep to rise if he should fall down in rugged terrain, so Jesus assists us to rise when we are overburdened or when the cross seems intolerably heavy. If we falter along the way, he carries us in his arms. (Lk 15:5).

He leads us safely through "the valley of darkness" to the fullness of divine life. "I came that they might have life, / and have it to the full" (Jn 10:10).

Like the shepherd, Jesus prepares a banquet for us, but one far more sumptuous. The banquet to which he invites us is the Eucharist in which he enriches and nourishes us along the way. Our cup is truly overflowing. The cup brimming over, which he offers us, was purchased at the price of his death.

With the psalmist we, too, say, "In the Lord's own house shall I dwell / forever and ever."

**The Life of the Church.** As we relive the liturgical cycle each year, we are aware that we are celebrating with the risen Jesus. He is dwelling within us through the power of his Spirit. This experience gives us a foretaste of our total union with him in heaven. This truth also reminds us of our own resurrection as the doorway into our eternal union.

Our focus, then, is always on the Good Shepherd who is leading us to our eternal destiny. This is his solemn promise: "Never again shall they know hunger or thirst/ nor shall the sun or its heat beat down on them/ for the Lamb on the throne will shepherd them/ He will lead them to springs of life-giving water, and God will wipe every tear from their eyes" (Rv 7:16f).

## *Psalm 121*
### *Providential Concern*

Our sojourn on earth is not simply a static state of patient waiting. It is, rather, a journey onward and upward, climaxing in the embrace of perfect love in our Father's arms.

Our journey may be fraught with many hardships, dangers, and temptations. Like any journey, we will have many needs as we travel along. However, we are never alone. Our provident God is accompanying us supplying our every need.

God is not a clockmaker, who creates us, winds us up, and then puts us on our own. On the contrary, he is always close by, watching over us with his bountiful, provident love.

In Psalm 121, the author recognizes his need for God. He knows that God's loving concern meets every need of his creatures. The psalmist appeals to us to always trust the Lord who is our guardian along life's highway.

With the psalmist, let us lift up our eyes to the mountain of the Lord as we contemplate his caring love.

*I lift up my eyes to the mountains;*
*from where shall come my help?*
*My help shall come from the Lord*
*who made heaven and earth.*

*May he never allow you to stumble!*
*Let him sleep not, your guard.*
*No, he sleeps not nor slumbers,*
*Israel's guard.*

*The Lord is your guard and your shade;*
*at your right side he stands.*
*By day the sun shall not smite you*
*nor the moon in the night.*

*The Lord will guard you from evil,*
*he will guard your soul.*
*The Lord will guard your going and coming*
*both now and for ever.*

**Reflections.** In the Psalter and throughout scripture, the tops of the mountains were considered the dwelling place of the Lord. "I lift up my eyes to the mountains."

The psalmist is so confident that God watches over and protects his people at all times that he continually reassures his companions of God's provident care. "May he never allow you to stumble."

Sunstrokes are common in Israel. There are

also many superstitions about the harmful effects of the moon. The psalmist was certainly aware of this fact and again declares that God will protect his people:

"By day the sun shall not smite you/ nor the moon in the night." "The Lord will guard your going and coming / both now and for ever." "Your going and coming" is an idiomatic expression to signify all ordinary human activity. God is concerned about every detail of a person's life. As the psalmist says elsewhere, "You mark when I walk or lie down / all my ways lie open to you" (Ps 139:3).

**The Life of Jesus.** Jesus dramatically manifested his providential care and concern for us as he joined the two disciples on the road to Emmaus. (Lk 24:13-35). He was concerned about their distress and discouragement. He wanted to encourage them and prevent them from becoming depressed and despondent.

As Jesus walked with the two, "he interpreted for them every passage of Scripture which referred to him." His elucidation was so clear that "they said to one another, 'Were not our hearts burning inside us as he talked to us on the road and explained the Scriptures to us?'" Only after the two disciples invited him to stay with them, did Jesus reveal himself to them in the breaking of the bread.

Each day Jesus accompanies us on the way to our own Emmaus. "Jesus Christ is the same yesterday, today and forever" (Heb 13:8). He speaks to us through his word. He nourishes us for our journey through the Eucharist.

This incident in the gospel perpetuates the assurance we received from the psalmist. Living with us in his resurrected life, Jesus continues to show us daily that he is our guardian, our provider, our companion on our journey back to the Father.

**The Life of the Church.** We are pilgrims on our way to the "New Jerusalem," our final destiny. "For here we have no lasting city; we are seeking one which is to come" (Heb 13:14).

Our pilgrimage may seem rough and arduous at times. We may feel faint and disheartened, but we know that our providential Father has taken care of all the logistics.

Even more, we are living with the risen Jesus who reminds us, "Apart from me you can do nothing" (Jn 15:5). What Jesus means is that with him we can do all things.

Furthermore, we know that we will certainly reach our destiny, because we know that the prayers of Jesus are always answered, and Jesus prayed, "I am in the world no more / but these are in the world / as I come to you. / O Father most holy / protect them with your name which you have given me / that they may be one, even as we are one . . . I do not ask you to take them out of the world / but to guard them from the evil one (Jn 17:11, 15).

Jesus all but guarantees that we will reach our journey's end safely when he assures us, "All you ask the Father in my name he will give you" (Jn 15:16). And again he says, "Whatever you ask in my name I will do, so as to glorify the Father in the Son. Anything you ask in my name I will do" (Jn 14:14).

## Psalm 111
### Praising God for His Goodness.

This psalm is one of the alphabet psalms written in acrostic style. Each half-line begins with a successive letter of the Hebrew alphabet, of which there are twenty-two.

As we might expect, there is no logical sequence to the words of this psalm. Rather, it is a series of reflections arising from the psalmist's meditation on the infinite goodness of God. As he ponders God's generosity, he is moved into a deep spirit of reverence. The awe and reverence which fills his heart makes him break forth into this song of thanksgiving and joy.

Our praying with the psalmist will bear much

fruit, enriching our own grateful response to God's overwhelming goodness.

*I will thank the Lord with all my heart*
*in the meeting of the just and their assembly.*
*Great are the works of the Lord;*
*to be pondered by all who love them.*

*Majestic and glorious his work,*
*his justice stands firm for ever.*
*He makes us remember his wonders.*
*The Lord is compassion and love.*

*He gives food to those who fear him;*
*keeps his covenant ever in mind.*
*He has shown his might to his people*
*by giving them the lands of the nations.*

*His works are justice and truth:*
*his precepts are all of them sure,*
*standing firm forever and ever:*
*they are made in uprightness and truth.*

*He has sent deliverance to his people*
*and established his covenant for ever.*
*Holy his name, to be feared.*

*To fear the Lord is the first stage of wisdom;*
*all who do so prove themselves wise.*
*His praise shall last for ever!*

**Reflections.** The psalmist is not only filled with gratitude himself, but he wants everyone to recognize God's goodness and praise him with all their hearts. This is why he speaks out in the assembly and meeting. "I will thank the Lord with all my heart / in the meeting of the just and their assembly."

As the writer contemplates God's "majestic and glorious work," he is overcome with a deep reverence and fear of the Lord.

While the psalmist's song of praise and thanksgiving embraces all God's beneficence, he does single out three specific areas of God's generosity. 1) He gives food to those who fear him. 2) The Lord supplies his people with food for both body and soul. 3) He has sent deliverance to his people.

God gave us his only Son as our Savior and Redeemer. Surely "the Lord is compassion and love." And he has established his covenant forever. Yes, God is faithful and will never break his part of his covenant with us.

Gratitude fills the psalmist's heart. He invites us to join him in praising and thanking God and to never cease doing so.

"His praise shall last forever!"

**The Life of Jesus.** In this, as in so many other ways, Jesus set an example which challenges us. Jesus continually thanked and praised his Father for his boundless goodness. "Father, Lord of heaven and earth, to you I offer praise. . . ." (Mt 11:25). "Jesus then took the loaves of bread, gave thanks. . . ." (Jn 6:11). "I have given you glory on earth by finishing the work you gave me to do" (Jn 17:4).

In his provident love, the Father sustained the Israelites with daily manna in the desert. Jesus implemented his providing love by giving us the gift of himself in the Eucharist. "I am the bread of life. / Your ancestors ate manna in the desert, but they died. / This is the bread that comes down from heaven / for a man to eat and never die. / I myself am the living bread / come down from heaven. / If anyone eats this bread / he shall live forever; / the bread I will give is my flesh, for the life of the world" (Jn 6:48ff).

In the Eucharist, Jesus bestowed the gift of himself in all his fullness upon us.

**The Life of the Church.** The inspired writer says, "To fear the Lord is the first stage of wisdom." In our modern parlance, we might use the expression: "To fear the Lord is to practice a religion."

The word "religion" means a relationship with God. We do have an innate sense of gratitude. When this gratitude is felt toward our provident Father, then we establish a personal relationship with him. Gratitude naturally characterizes our relationship with God, to whom we owe everything we are and have.

In giving us the Holy Eucharist, Jesus instituted an ideal way in which we can express our gratitude to our generous and gracious God. When we offer the Eucharist, Jesus accepts the gift of ourselves with all that we are and do, and gives it to the Father in our name. This adds a divine dimension to our praise and thanksgiving to the Father.

The night on which Jesus gave us the Eucharist, he also said, "My Father has been glorified / in your bearing much fruit / and becoming my disciples" (Jn 15:8).

If we may paraphrase the words of the psalmist:

To offer our praise and thanks to the Lord
is the first stage of wisdom;
all who do so prove themselves wise.
His praise shall last for ever! (vs 10).

Let us pray:

Mighty and wonderful are your works
Lord God Almighty!
Righteous and true are your ways,
O King of the nations!
Who would dare refuse you honor,
or the glory due your name, O Lord?
Since you alone are holy,
all nations shall come
and worship in your presence.
Your mighty deeds are clearly seen (Rv 15:3f).

# FIVE

# Merciful Love

## Psalm 130
### Cry for Mercy

THE SIXTH PENITENTIAL PSALM is a fervent prayer for forgiveness. Distressed by his own sinfulness, the psalmist humbly seeks forgiveness both for himself and for the community. Even though he is plagued by his own infidelities, he trusts in the mercy of the Lord.

Sometimes this psalm is applied to an individual or to all of exiled Israel. The psalm's deliverance would be only a partial redemption while Israel waited for the full redemption which Jesus brought.

Since we, too, are sinners, let us join our plea for forgiveness with the psalmist.

*Out of the depths I cry to you, O Lord,*
*Lord, hear my voice!*
*O let your ears be attentive*
*to the voice of my pleading.*

*If you, O Lord, should mark our guilt,*
*Lord, who would survive?*
*But with you is found forgiveness:*
*for this we revere you.*

*My soul is waiting for the Lord,*
*I count on his word.*
*My soul is longing for the Lord*
*more than watchman for daybreak.*
*Let the watchman count on daybreak*
*and Israel on the Lord.*

*Because with the Lord there is mercy*
*and fullness of redemption,*
*Israel indeed he will redeem*
*from all its iniquity.*

**Reflections.** Experiencing great spiritual misery and moved to genuine sorrow, the psalmist cries out for forgiveness: "Out of the depths I cry to you, O Lord."

Realizing that God is all-merciful, the psalmist is comforted as he says to the Lord, "With you is found forgiveness."

The author repeats his trust in the compassionate and merciful love of God: "My soul is waiting for the Lord, I count on his word."

We, too, come before the Lord confidently and contritely "because with the Lord there is mercy and fullness of redemption."

**The Life of Jesus.** Even at his birth, Jesus was hailed as the Savior who came to forgive: "I come to proclaim good news to you—tidings of great joy to be shared by the whole people. This day in David's city a savior has been born to you, the Messiah and Lord" (Lk 2:10f).

Just a few days later Simeon also hailed the coming of the Redeemer: "For my eyes have witnessed your saving deed displayed for all the people to see" (Lk 2:30).

Jesus proclaimed himself Savior and Redeemer: "The Son of Man has not come to be served but to serve—to give his life in ransom for the many" (Mk 10:45).

Like the psalmist, our trust is greatly increased when we hear Jesus assure us: "I have come to call sinners, not the self-righteous" (Mk 2:17).

**The Life of the Church.** This prayer for pardon and mercy is used in the liturgy of the church as a prayer for the faithful departed. We pray it many times in the Liturgy of the Hours also. As we pray this psalm, we recall St. Paul's rhetorical question: "Do you not know that God's kindness is an invitation to you to repent?" (Rom 2:4).

Jesus won our salvation, but we often still need to call out for mercy, pardon, and forgiveness. If our prayer is constant, we will also be comforted.

As pilgrims, this is our psalm.

## Psalm 51
### Conditioning for Forgiveness

Psalm 51 is the finest and best-known of the penitential psalms. It was composed by a sinner who experienced the gravity of his own sinfulness. He cannot rest until he knows he is forgiven. He confesses his sinfulness sincerely and longs to be completely purified.

The psalmist stands before God as a sinner. He is painfully aware of his guilt, but not afraid. In fact, he sees his sin as a claim to God's mercy, the source of his hope.

As we pray this psalm, our sense of guilt unites us with God, who eagerly desires to forgive us. Aware of God's great compassion, we accept the outpouring of his infinite mercy. And with the psalmist we promise, "My mouth shall declare your praise."

*Have mercy on me, God, in your kindness.*
*In your compassion blot out my offense.*
*O wash me more and more from my guilt*
*and cleanse me from my sin.*

*My offenses truly I know them;*
*my sin is always before me.*
*Against you, you alone, have I sinned;*
*what is evil in your sight I have done.*

*That you may be justified when you give sentence*

*and be without reproach when you judge.*
*O see, in guilt I was born,*
*a sinner was I conceived.*

*Indeed you love truth in the heart;*
*then in the secret of my heart teach me wisdom.*
*O purify me, then I shall be clean;*
*O wash me, I shall be whiter than snow.*

*Make me hear rejoicing and gladness,*
*that the bones you have crushed may revive.*
*From my sins turn away your face*
*and blot out all my guilt.*

*A pure heart create for me, O God,*
*put a steadfast spirit within me.*
*Do not cast me away from your presence,*
*nor deprive me of your holy spirit.*

*Give me again the joy of your help;*
*with a spirit of fervor sustain me,*
*that I may teach transgressors your ways*
*and sinners may return to you.*

*O rescue me, God, my helper,*
*and my tongue shall ring out your goodness.*
*O Lord, open my lips*
*and my mouth shall declare your praise.*

*For in sacrifice you take no delight,*
*burnt offering from me you would refuse,*
*my sacrifice, a contrite spirit.*
*A humbled, contrite heart you will not spurn.*

*In your goodness, show favor to Zion:*
*rebuild the walls of Jerusalem.*
*Then you will be pleased with lawful sacrifice,*
*holocausts offered on your altar.*

**Reflections.** As the psalmist prays earnestly for God's mercy and for a purified heart, he touches upon an essential condition for obtaining mercy—a recognition of the need for God's gracious forgiveness: "Have mercy on me, God, in your kindness. / In your compassion blot out my offense."

This recognition and acknowledgment of sinfulness is a major step toward forgiveness. "My offenses truly I know them." The inspired writer recognizes our broken human nature: "In guilt I was born, a sinner was I conceived." This expression could be a foreshadowing of the Christian doctrine of original sin.

After having been forgiven, the psalmist promises to make God's mercy and compassion known to others. He will sing the praises of the Lord to everyone: "My mouth shall declare your praise."

God desires only one gift, and that is the gift of ourselves. As we die to self, we are able to offer God a humbled, contrite heart. "My sacrifice, a contrite spirit. / A humbled, contrite heart you will not spurn."

**The Life of Jesus.** The gospel message is often an

encouragement, if not an urgent call, to be receptive to the merciful forgiveness of the Lord. St. John the Baptist's teaching is brief but to the point: "Reform your lives! The reign of God is at hand" (Mk 3:2).

John's mission is similarly described: "He went about the entire region of the Jordan proclaiming a baptism of repentance which led to the forgiveness of sins" (Lk 3:3).

Jesus went much further than the psalmist. He taught us to call God our Father. He described the image of the Father in the father of the prodigal son. The father ran out to meet his son. He did not wait for an explanation, or confession, or even an apology, but he took him into his arms and kissed him.

The wayward son had already repented in his own heart. "Coming to his senses" he resolved, "I will break away and return to my father, and say to him, 'Father, I have sinned against God and against you; I no longer deserve to be called your son'" (Lk 15:17).

Like the prodigal son, we, too, must recognize and acknowledge our sinfulness as we approach our compassionate Father. This is the first step on the way to pardon and peace.

*Love* instinctively responds to *love* with confidence, trust, and humility. Jesus compels us to seek his merciful forgiveness when he tells us: "There is no greater love than this: to lay down one's life for one's friends" (Jn 15:13).

Such love brings into focus our own sinfulness and encourages us to appeal for forgiveness with the confidence and trust that we will be pardoned.

**The Life of the Church.** In the penitential rite of the Mass, as we stand in the brilliance of the Lord's presence, we recognize our own unworthiness and plead for God's mercy. This plea grows throughout the Eucharistic Celebration until it breaks forth in the Lord's Prayer.

In the time of Jesus, rabbis often incorporated a summary of their teaching in a prayer form. In teaching us the Our Father, Jesus did the same. He taught us how we must prepare ourselves to receive the Lord's forgiveness.

As we pray, "forgive us our trespasses as we forgive those who trespass against us," we express our desire to forgive all who have harmed us. In doing so, we, too, may be less unworthy of his mercy and compassion.

Who of us can comprehend the boundless love and compassion of so merciful a God?

## Psalm 32
### *Joy in Forgiveness*

All of us sin and occasionally inflict pain on another person. Such instances probably make us feel guilty and disappointed in ourselves.

However, if in humility and without "guile" we

are able to apologize to the person and receive forgiveness, peace again returns to us. If the offended person not only forgives us, but accepts us once again as a close friend, our hearts are filled with joy.

We can experience the same joy in an even greater measure in our relationship with our loving Father. This is the special message of Psalm 32. Even though it is listed as a penitential psalm, the mood is more one of joy rather than penance.

*Happy the man whose offense is forgiven,*
*whose sin is remitted.*
*O happy the man to whom the Lord*
*imputes no guilt,*
*in whose spirit is no guile.*

*I kept it secret and my frame was wasted.*
*I groaned all the day long*
*for night and day your hand*
*was heavy upon me.*
*Indeed, my strength was dried up*
*as by the summer's heat.*

*But now I have acknowledged my sins;*
*my guilt I did not hide.*
*I said: "I will confess*
*my offense to the Lord."*
*And you, Lord, have forgiven*
*the guilt of my sin.*

*So let every good man pray to you*
*in time of need.*
*The floods of water may reach high*
*but him they shall not reach.*
*You are my hiding place, O Lord;*
*you save me from distress.*
*You surround me with cries of deliverance.*

*I will instruct you and teach you*
*the way you should go;*
*I will give you counsel*
*with my eye upon you.*

*Be not like the horse and mule, unintelligent,*
*needing bridle and bit,*
*else they will not approach you.*
*Many sorrows has the wicked*
*but he who trusts in the Lord,*
*loving mercy surrounds him.*

*Rejoice, rejoice in the Lord,*
*exult, you just!*
*O come, ring out your joy,*
*all you upright of heart.*

**Reflections.** Psalm 32 contains many lessons. The author assures us that a virtuous life is by no means a gloomy one. Happiness awaits the repentant sinner. "Happy the man whose offense is forgiven / whose sin is remitted."

At first the psalmist wanted to keep his guilt a secret, but found great torment in harboring it in his own heart. Gradually he discovered he could no longer deny his sinfulness, but had to admit his infidelity openly: "I kept it secret and my frame was wasted."

In suffering, he recognized the malice of his sin and the necessity for acknowledging it. His admission brought him pardon. When confession follows acknowledgment, there is real spiritual consolation and joy.

St. Augustine tells us that even before a sin is verbally confessed, God hears the cry of the heart. Forgiveness always follows sincere confession.

David experienced this same merciful forgiveness after he acknowledged his sin. "Then David said to Nathan, 'I have sinned against the Lord.' Nathan answered David: 'The Lord on his part has forgiven your sin; you shall not die'" (1 Sm 12:13).

When the psalmist experienced great joy after receiving forgiveness, he wanted to share it with others and encouraged them to turn to the Lord. He insisted, "I will instruct you and teach you the way you should go."

In contrast to the misery of those who do evil and remain unrepentant, there is great joy awaiting those who seek forgiveness: "Rejoice in the Lord . . . ring out your joy."

God wants us to be happy and rejoice. He will lead us to "ring out our joy." If we are willing, the Lord will do the rest.

**The Life of Jesus.** Jesus told a story pointing out the need for us to admit our sinfulness. Both a Pharisee and a tax collector went to the Temple to pray. Humbly, the tax collector confessed his sinfulness and sought forgiveness: "O God, be merciful to me a sinner." On the other hand, the Pharisee admitted no guilt and no reason for asking for pardon. Jesus' comment is both consoling and tragic. Speaking of the tax collector Jesus said, "This man went home from the temple justified but the other did not" (Lk 18:9ff).

Forgiveness always brings great joy even in heaven. "I tell you, there will likewise be more joy in heaven over one repentant sinner than over ninety-nine righteous people who have no need to repent" (Lk 15:70).

In the parable of the prodigal son, the father, who represents our heavenly Father, explained to his elder son the reason for the celebration. "We had to celebrate and rejoice! This brother of yours was dead, and has come back to life. He was lost and is found" (Lk 15:32).

**The Life of the Church.** In the work of sanctification, the Holy Spirit reinforces our hope of salvation: "God has not destined us for wrath but for acquiring salvation through our Lord Jesus

Christ. He died for us, that all of us, whether awake or asleep, together might live with him" (1 Thes 5:9).

The Spirit reiterated this truth in scripture: "He rescued us from the power of darkness and brought us into the kingdom of his beloved son. Through him we have redemption, the forgiveness of our sins" (Col 1:13f).

Jesus wanted to assure each one of us that he personally forgives us through the Sacrament of Penance. The very day he rose from the dead, Jesus empowered his first priests to forgive sins. He had just redeemed us and he now wanted that forgiveness imparted immediately through the rite of reconciliation: "Receive the Holy Spirit, / If you forgive men's sins, / they are forgiven them; / if you hold them bound, / they are held bound" (Jn 20:22f).

This sacrament is rightly called the source of our joy!

# SIX

# Redemptive Love

## Psalm 22
## Suffering Servant

WE NEED TO CONTEMPLATE the passion and death of Jesus frequently for our spiritual growth and maturation. Psalm 22 can nurture in us a great sense of gratitude for the death Jesus suffered for our sins. Gratitude is proportionate to the worth of the gift. Jesus could not have given more.

When we begin to realize the humiliating suffering Jesus underwent for us, we are moved to have greater compassion for our brothers and sisters throughout the world.

When we contemplate the love which impelled Jesus to lay down his life for us, our own love for him will mature. Nothing can increase our love for Jesus more than our reflection on his prophetic words: "There is no greater love than this: to lay down one's life for one's friends" (Jn 15:13).

Psalm 22 is one of the most important messianic psalms. The opening words of the psalm are the seven last words spoken by Jesus as he hung on the cross. Several other verses are quoted or alluded to in the New Testament.

This prayer can be divided into two parts. The first twenty-two verses describe the anguish of the Suffering Servant. The physical and spiritual sufferings recounted here reflect those experienced in the passion of Jesus. The second section describes the victory and triumph of the Messiah as well as the fruits of the redemption.

A very ill person may whisper the initial words of a familiar prayer, such as the "Our Father," and then let his thoughts finish the rest of the prayer. Jesus might have done so as he hung on the cross and prayed, "My God, my God, why have you forsaken me."

With Jesus let us pray this psalm.

*My God, my God, why have you forsaken me?*
*You are far from my plea and the cry of my distress.*
*O my God, I call by day and you give no reply;*
*I call by night and I find no peace.*

*Yet you, O God, are holy,*
*enthroned on the praises of Israel.*
*In you our fathers put their trust;*
*they trusted and you set them free.*
*When they cried to you, they escaped.*
*In you they trusted and never in vain.*

*But I am a worm and no man,*

*scorned by men, despised by the people.*
*All who see me deride me.*
*They curl their lips, they toss their heads.*
*"He trusted in the Lord, let him save him;*
*let him release him if this is his friend."*

*Yes, it was you who took me from the womb,*
*entrusted me to my mother's breast.*
*To you I was committed from my birth,*
*from my mother's womb you have been my God.*
*Do not leave me alone in my distress;*
*come close, there is none else to help.*

*Many bulls have surrounded me,*
*fierce bulls of Bashan close me in.*
*Against me they open wide their jaws,*
*like lions, rending and roaring.*

*Like water I am poured out,*
*disjointed are all my bones.*
*My heart has become like wax,*
*it is melted within my breast.*

*Parched as burnt clay is my throat,*
*my tongue cleaves to my jaws.*

*Many dogs have surrounded me,*
*a band of the wicked beset me.*
*They tear holes in my hands and my feet*
*and lay me in the dust of death.*

*I can count every one of my bones.*
*These people stare at me and gloat;*

they divide my clothing among them.
They cast lots for my robe.

O Lord, do not leave me alone,
my strength, make haste to help me!
Rescue my soul from the sword,
my life from the grip of these dogs.
Save my life from the jaws of these lions,
my poor soul from the horns of these oxen.

I will tell of your name to my brethren
and praise you where they are assembled.

"You who fear the Lord, give him praise;
all sons of Jacob, give him glory.
Revere him, Israel's sons.

For he has never despised
nor scorned the poverty of the poor.
From him he has not hidden his face,
but he heard the poor man when he cried."

You are my praise in the great assembly.
My vows I will pay before those who fear him.
The poor shall eat and shall have their fill.
They shall praise the Lord, those who seek him.
May their hearts live for ever and ever!

All the earth shall remember and return to the
    Lord,
all families of the nations worship before him
for the kingdom is the Lord's; he is ruler of the
    nations.

*They shall worship him, all the mighty of the earth;*
*before him shall bow all who go down to the dust.*

*And my soul shall live for him, my children serve*
*    him.*
*They shall tell of the Lord to generations yet to*
*    come,*
*declare his faithfulness to peoples yet unborn:*
*"These things the Lord has done."*

**Reflections.** The psalmist tries to describe in figurative language the extent and severity of his sufferings.

"They curl their lips, they toss their heads." Curled lips is a manner of sneering, expressing utter contempt and disdain. Likewise, tossing the head is a gesture of derision.

"Fierce bulls of Bashan close me in." Bashan was a rich grazing land east of the Jordan. It was well known for its large and strong cattle. Here it is used to describe the power and the strength of the enemies attacking the psalmist. Such expressions as "dogs," "lions," "oxen," are metaphors. These fierce animals signify the cruelty of the psalmist's persecutors.

Beginning with verse 23, there is a sudden and clear-cut transition to a hymn of thanksgiving for the saving power of God.

The psalmist closes with an assurance that all generations yet to come shall declare the faithfulness of the Lord.

**The Life of Jesus.** Psalm 22 describes the suffering and deliverance that was perfectly fulfilled in Jesus. The gospel takes up the words of the psalmist in recording the sufferings of Jesus. As we pray this psalm, these parallels become apparent.

Jesus himself prayed the words of this psalm from his deathbed on the cross: "My God, my God, why have you forsaken me?" (Mt 27:46).

The psalmist describes the rejection of the Suffering Servant in these words: "All who see me deride me, / they curl their lips, they toss their heads."

We recognize this type of rejection in Matthew's description of the crucifixion of Jesus: "People going by kept insulting him, tossing their heads and saying: 'So you are the one who was going to destroy the temple and rebuild it in three days! Come down off that cross if you are God's Son!'" (Mt 27:39f).

The psalmist continues to describe the kind of derision which the Messiah would have to endure: "He trusted in the Lord, let him save him; / let him release him if this is his friend."

The chief priests, the scribes, and the elders voiced this same ridicule to Jesus as he hung on the cross: "He relied on God; let God rescue him now if he wants to. After all he claimed, 'I am God's Son.'" (Mt 27:43).

The feverish pain of thirst can be excruciating. Experiencing this kind of suffering, the psalmist cried out, "Parched as burnt clay is my throat, / my tongue cleaves to my jaws."

In his dying moments, Jesus whispered in a weakening voice, "I am thirsty." "There was a jar there, full of common wine. They stuck a sponge soaked in this wine on some hyssop and raised it to his lips."

This terrible thirst was one of the last sufferings Jesus endured: "When Jesus took the wine, he said, 'Now it is finished.' Then he bowed his head, and delivered over his spirit" (Jn 19:28ff).

The psalmist presents another detail which is also recorded in the New Testament: "They divided my clothing among them. / They cast lots for my robe."

The evangelist describes this happening in these words:

> After the soldiers had crucified Jesus they took his garments and divided them in four ways, one for each soldier. There was also a tunic, but this tunic was woven in one piece from top to bottom and had no seam. They said to each other, "We should not tear it. (The purpose of this was to have the Scripture fulfilled: "They divided my garments among them; for my clothing they cast lots.")" (Jn 19:23ff).

The significance in this recorded fact is that the tunics of the priests were always "one piece from top to bottom and had no seam." This characterized Jesus as a true priest, and many recognized him as the high priest of the new dispensation. Furthermore, he offered himself on the cross at the same hour in which the paschal lambs were being slain in the Temple for the great feast of Passover.

**The Life of the Church.** In the liturgy, the church relives with the risen Jesus his cruel sufferings and death, but is ever mindful that his sufferings were his glorification and our salvation.

The second portion of Psalm 22 is a hymn of triumph. In the Easter liturgy, the church takes up this refrain by echoing and reechoing Jesus' victory over sin and death in the "Alleluia" chant of joy.

St. Paul continually reminds us of the victory of Jesus' resurrection. "It is in Christ and through his blood that we have been redeemed and our sins forgiven, so immeasurably generous is God's favor to us. . . ." (Eph 1:7ff).

He continues:

God is rich in mercy; because of his great love for us he brought us to life with Christ when we were dead in sin. By this favor you were saved. . . . I repeat, it is owing to his favor that salvation is yours through faith. This is not your doing, it is God's gift; neither is it a reward for anything you have accomplished, so let no one pride himself on it (Eph 2:4ff).

## *Psalm 56*
### *Trust in Adversity*

This psalm portrays the sufferings Jesus endured in his passion. He suffered to show us the way and to encourage us to trust, even though we cannot understand the mystery of suffering.

As we make the psalmist's prayer our own, we begin to understand that God permits pain, suffering, and sorrow in our lives in order to purify us, to strengthen us, and to help us mature spiritually.

Even though suffering is shrouded in mystery, we know that it does have a purpose in our lives. It will eventually bring us to the point that we "may walk in the presence of God and enjoy the light of the living." This gives us the hope and trust we need to dispel all fear.

With a listening heart let us pray with the psalmist.

*Have mercy on me, God, men crush me;*
*they fight me all day long and oppress me.*
*My foes crush me all day long,*
*for many fight proudly against me.*
*When I fear, I will trust in you,*
*in God whose word I praise.*

*In God I trust, I shall not fear:*
*what can mortal man do to me?*

*All day long they distort my words,*
*all their thought is to harm me.*
*They band together in ambush,*
*track me down and seek my life.*
*You have kept an account of my wanderings;*
*you have kept a record of my tears;*
*are they not written in your book?*

*Then my foes will be put to flight*
*on the day that I call to you.*
*This I know, that God is on my side.*
*In God, whose word I praise,*
*in the Lord, whose word I praise,*
*in God I trust; I shall not fear:*
*what can mortal man do to me?*

*I am bound by the vows I have made you.*
*O God, I will offer you praise*
*for you rescued my soul from death,*
*you kept my feet from stumbling*
*that I may walk in the presence of God*
*and enjoy the light of the living.*

**Reflections.** After the psalmist's plea, "have mercy on me, God," his fear is removed because he trusts in God: "When I fear, I will trust in you, / in God, whose word I praise. / In God I trust; I shall not fear: / what can mortal man do to me?"

The psalmist uses another expression which

may seem a little unusual to us: "You have kept a record of my tears; / are they not written in your book?"

In the psalmist's day, professional mourners were hired at the time of the death of a loved one. These mourners collected their tears in a bottle and left them at the grave of the deceased. The amount of tears was an indication of how much the person was loved.

We have no need to collect our tears, because our loving Father is aware of all the pain and sorrow we endure. Our tears may not be written in his book, but we can be certain they are never shed in vain.

In verses 10-12, the writer reiterates his trust in the Lord. "In God I trust; I shall not fear."

Because of the suffering of Jesus, all our pains and hardships are redemptive. They have a purpose in our lives and will lead us eventually to "walk in the presence of God and enjoy the light of the living."

This is the New Jerusalem—heaven—for which we are all bound.

**The Life of Jesus.** We know of several occasions when Jesus wept in public. One such occasion was the time he saw Martha weeping at the death of her brother, Lazarus. Jesus himself was overcome. "Jesus began to weep" (Jn 11:33ff).

During his messianic entry into Jerusalem on Palm Sunday, Jesus could not restrain his tears as he thought of the fate of the Holy City and its unfaithful people. "Coming within sight of the city, he wept over it" (Lk 19:41).

Jesus redeemed our human nature which enables us to be united with him for all eternity. In describing the new heaven and the new earth, St. John writes:

> This is God's dwelling among men. He shall dwell with them and they shall be his people and he shall be their God who is always with them. He shall wipe every tear from their eyes, and there shall be no more death or mourning, crying out or pain for the former world has passed away (Rv 21:3).

By virtue of Jesus' sufferings, our pain and sorrow is redemptive, and will enable us to "enjoy the light of the living."

With the psalmist we, too, can say: "In God I trust; I shall not fear."

**The Life of the Church.** There are many kinds of tears. In pain and suffering, tears may flow uncontrollably. Anger, frustration, and rejection may also cause tears to flow. And when we begin to comprehend God's bountiful goodness, tears of joy may well up within us and flow freely.

We also speak of tears as a special gift from God. Tears may accompany an enriching time of prayer.

When the Holy Spirit envelops our spirit, he breaks down all the inhibitions which often restrict us. As the Spirit is released within us, tears of joy and exultation may flow generously without our willing it.

If the psalmist, in the midst of his suffering, had reason to place his hope and trust in God, how much greater should be our faith and confidence as we contemplate the sufferings of Jesus.

Then we can truly say: "Father, 'when I fear, I will trust in you.'"

## Psalm 102
### Grief-Stricken yet Confident

This psalm is the prayer of an exile expressing his loneliness and his longing for the presence of the Lord in the Temple.

Loneliness is one of the greatest afflictions of our times. We, too, are exiles in this land of sojourn. Nothing in this life can fully satisfy the longing of the human heart. The only genuine remedy for loneliness is a deeper, more personal relationship with our loving Father and with Jesus living within us.

We may experience loneliness when we stray far from the Lord, or when we become too engrossed with self, or with the mundane life surrounding us. The Lord may permit us to experience an emptiness—a loneliness—in order to bring us back to him. God permitted the Israelites to be dragged into exile when they strayed away from the way of life he asked them to follow. He may do the same with us.

*O Lord, listen to my prayer*
*and let my cry for help reach you.*
*Do not hide your face from me*
*in the day of my distress.*
*Turn your ear towards me*
*and answer me quickly when I call.*

*For my days are vanishing like smoke,*
*My bones burn away like a fire.*
*My heart is withered like the grass.*
*I forget to eat my bread.*
*I cry with all my strength*
*and my skin clings to my bones.*

*I have become like a pelican in the wilderness,*
*like an owl in desolate places.*
*I lie awake and I moan*
*like some lonely bird on a roof.*
*All day long my foes revile me;*
*those who hate me use my name as a curse.*

*The bread I eat is ashes;*
*my drink is mingled with tears.*
*In your anger, Lord, and your fury*
*you have lifted me up and thrown me down.*
*My days are like a passing shadow*
*and I wither away like the grass.*

But you, O Lord, will endure for ever
and your name from age to age.
You will arise and have mercy on Zion:
for this is the time to have mercy:
yes, the time appointed has come
for your servants love her very stones,
are moved with pity even for her dust.

The nations shall fear the name of the Lord
and all the earth's kings your glory,
when the Lord shall build up Zion again
and appear in all his glory.
Then he will turn to the prayers of the helpless;
he will not despise their prayers.

Let this be written for ages to come
that a people yet unborn may praise the Lord;
for the Lord leaned down from his sanctuary on
    high.
He looked down from heaven to the earth
that he might hear the groans of the prisoners
and free those condemned to die.

The sons of your servants shall dwell untroubled
and their race shall endure before you
that the name of the Lord may be proclaimed in
    Zion
and his praise in the heart of Jerusalem,
when the people and kingdoms are gathered
    together
to pay their homage to the Lord.

He has broken my strength in mid-course;
he has shortened the days of my life.

*I say to God: "Do not take me away*
*before my days are complete,*
*you whose days last from age to age.*

*Long ago you founded the earth*
*and the heavens are the work of your hands.*
*They will perish but you will remain.*
*They will wear out like a garment.*
*You will change them like clothes that are changed.*
*But you neither change, nor have an end."*

**Reflections.** The psalmist's opening words, "O Lord, listen to my prayer," are a fervent prayer of a person who is lonely, ill, seemingly abandoned by everyone, especially by God. He pleads with the Lord not to turn a deaf ear to his prayer.

His expressions reflect his state of mind. The psalmist feels "like a pelican in the wilderness" and "like an owl in desolate places." The wilderness and desolate places are not the natural habitats for either the pelican or the owl. Like them, the psalmist imagines himself in the midst of a desert wasteland. Such an environment would certainly contribute to the pain of loneliness.

In verses 13 to 19, his prayer is filled with faith, hope, and the expectation of God coming to aid him. Addressing the Lord, he says: "You will arise and have mercy on Zion: / for this is the time to have mercy."

And he continues with these reassuring words: "Then he will turn to the prayers of the helpless; / he will not despise their prayers."

In verses 19-23, the people are invited to "pay their homage to the Lord" because: "He looked down from heaven to the earth / that he might hear the groans of the prisoners / and free those condemned to die."

The conclusion of this psalm is a song of praise to the Lord extolling his goodness. In praising God, the psalmist says: "But you neither change, nor have an end."

**The Life of Jesus.** Jesus knew how lonely we would be far from our home in heaven. Therefore he promised us: "I will not leave you orphaned; / I will come back to you" (Jn 14:18).

In Matthew's gospel, Jesus reassures us, "And know that I am with you always, / until the end of the world" (Mt 28:20).

Jesus knew that we would often wonder about his presence with us and within us. Once again he promised: "Anyone who loves me / will be true to my word, / and my Father will love him; / we will come to him / and make our dwelling place with him" (Jn 14:23).

The divine presence within us is a mystery. In his divine wisdom, Jesus had the facility of explaining a mystery with a figure of speech that would satisfy our curiosity and help us to accept it in faith. In this instance, he told us the allegory of the vine and the branches (Jn 15:1-8).

While this figure of speech does not adequately explain his mysterious presence, it does give us some insights which help us to be more aware of his abiding presence within us.

**The Life of the Church.** In the Rite of Initiation, the church reminds us that we are the temples of the Holy Spirit, who is not merely a guest but remains with us permanently. God says, "I will dwell with them and walk among them. / I will be their God / and they shall be my people. . . . / I will welcome you and be a father to you / and you will be my sons and daughters" (2 Cor 6:16ff).

In his *Confessions,* St. Augustine relates his experience of loneliness and tells where he found the solution.

Late have I loved you. O Beauty ever ancient, ever new, late have I loved you! You were within me, but I was outside, and it was there that I searched for you. In my unloveliness I plunged into the lovely things which you created. You were with me, but I was not with you. Created things kept me far from you; yet if they had not been in you they would not have been at all. You called, you shouted, and you broke through my deafness. You flashed, you shone, and you dispelled my blindness. You breathed your fragrance on me, I drew in breath and now I pant for you. I have tasted you; now I hunger and thirst for more. You touched me, and I burned for your peace.

(Liturgy of the Hours III p. 273)

As we ponder St. Augustine's words as well as the prayer of the psalmist, we will find remedy for loneliness.

As the psalmist prays for Zion, let us pray for the church that all our brothers and sisters may find comfort in "the God of all consolation."

"He comforts us in all our afflictions and thus enables us to comfort those who are in trouble, with the same consolation we have received from him" (2 Cor 1:4).

# SEVEN

# Gratitude

## Psalm 103
### God's Tender Compassion

A DEDICATED FOLLOWER OF JESUS will always reflect a grateful heart. Gratitude wells up naturally in our heart when we pause to count our blessings. On the other hand, an ungrateful person can hardly radiate the image of Jesus.

Psalm 103 is a hymn of praise and thanksgiving for all God's goodness. It is a tender expression praising the Lord for his boundless generosity.

The psalmist begins with his own expression of praise, then realizing that his praise is inadequite, he calls upon all the servants and hosts of the Lord to assist him in extolling such a good God.

The psalmist is especially appreciative of God's forgiving love. As we pray this hymn with the psalmist, we can ponder and reflect upon God's goodness to each one of us.

My soul, give thanks to the Lord,
all my being, bless his holy name.
My soul, give thanks to the Lord
and never forget all his blessings.

It is he who forgives all your guilt,
who heals every one of your ills,
who redeems your life from the grave,
who crowns you with love and compassion,
who fills your life with good things,
renewing your youth like an eagle's.

The Lord does deeds of justice,
gives judgment for all who are oppressed.
He made known his ways to Moses
and his deeds to Israel's sons.

The Lord is compassion and love,
slow to anger and rich in mercy.
His wrath will come to an end;
he will not be angry for ever.
He does not treat us according to our sins
nor repay us according to our faults.

For as the heavens are high above the earth
so strong is his love for those who fear him.
As far as the east is from the west
so far does he remove our sins.

As a father has compassion on his sons,
the Lord has pity on those who fear him;

*for he knows of what we are made,*
*he remembers that we are dust.*

*As for man, his days are like grass;*
*he flowers like the flower of the field;*
*the wind blows and he is gone*
*and his place never sees him again.*

*But the love of the Lord is everlasting*
*upon those who hold him in fear;*
*his justice reaches out to children's children*
*when they keep his covenant in truth,*
*when they keep his will in their mind.*

*The Lord has set his sway in heaven*
*and his kingdom is ruling over all.*
*Give thanks to the Lord, all his angels,*
*mighty in power, fulfilling his word,*
*who heed the voice of his word.*

*Give thanks to the Lord, all his hosts,*
*his servants who do his will.*
*Give thanks to the Lord all his works,*
*in every place where he rules.*
*My soul, give thanks to the Lord!*

**Reflections.** God's love is so infinite that the psalmist cannot comprehend it. He considers its various facets. He rejoices because the Lord "forgives, heals, and redeems" in spite of man's sinfulness. "It is he who forgives all your guilt."

To "forgive" means that he wipes away sin. To "heal" is to remove a sense of guilt and the wounds left by sin. His redemptive love brings good out of every failing. He does not approve the sin, but he can use it for our good.

The author sings the goodness of the Lord: "Who crowns you with love and compassion / who fills your life with good things."

Because the Lord loves us so much, he wants to offer forgiveness even more than we desire to seek it. That, too, is a mystery.

"As a father has compassion on his sons, / the Lord has pity on those who fear him." This is a very touching comparison, but the psalmist does not yet dare to call God, Father. Only after Jesus revealed God as our loving, caring Father would anyone dare to call God, Father. Jesus even taught us to pray "Our Father . . ."

The psalmist is overwhelmed by the abundance of God's goodness. Feeling inadequate, he calls upon all the hosts of heaven and the servants of the Lord to praise and thank the Lord for him. He then concludes with his own word of thanksgiving: "My soul, give thanks to the Lord!"

**The Life of Jesus.** Jesus witnessed to his own teachings by putting into practice what he taught. He urges us to praise the Father and also to be grateful at all times. "On one occasion Jesus spoke thus: 'Father, Lord of heaven and earth, to you I offer praise; for what you have hidden from the learned and the clever you have revealed to the merest children'" (Mt 11:25).

And again: "Jesus then took the loaves of bread, gave thanks . . ." (Jn 6:11).

And again: "Father, I thank you for having heard me" (Jn 11:41).

In the Sermon on the Mount, Jesus urges us to show the same mercy and compassion for our enemies which the Father shows us: "My command to you is: love your enemies, pray for your persecutors. . . . In a word, you must be made perfect as your heavenly Father is perfect" (Mt 5:43ff).

**The Life of the Church.** The life of a Christian must radiate the joy of the Lord. One of the many reasons for our joy is our awareness of God's boundless generosity. As the psalmist says, God is higher than the heavens, yet he is very close to us in his love and mercy. Jesus came not only to redeem us, but to remain with us. He loves us so much that he abides with us and within us in his glorified, risen life.

One of the most powerful ways in which we can thank the Lord is through the Eucharistic Celebration. This celebration is a perfect act of thanksgiving because Jesus takes our thanks and unites it with his own thanksgiving to the Father. This adds a divine dimension to our thanks.

In the Eucharist, Jesus loves us so much that he comes to remain with us. As we contemplate his divine goodness and graciousness, our hearts, like that of the psalmist, want to break forth in a hymn of praise and thanksgiving.

Like the psalmist, we cannot thank the Lord adequately; hence we not only call upon the court of heaven to join us, but we ask Jesus himself to lift our praise and thanks to the throne of the Father.

## Psalm 65
### Hymn of Thanksgiving

God endowed each one of us with a sense of gratitude. Gratitude is an inherent quality in our human nature. Our sense of gratitude will be, first of all, directed toward God who has abundantly blessed each one of us and, secondly, to all those who show us kindness and concern.

Aside from gratitude, we have probably experienced the pain of ingratitude. Perhaps we have been generous with our time and effort at great personal sacrifice only to be ignored or rejected by the person we tried to help. We experienced disappointment and heartache.

Our indebtedness to our loving Father is beyond comprehension. Even a momentary reflection on his goodness astounds us. When we consider his lavish gifts, words often fail us. The words of the psalmist direct our heart and our prayer to some of the areas of God's gracious providence.

Let us pray with him:

*To you our praise is due*
*in Zion, O God.*
*To you we pay our vows,*
*you who hear our prayer.*

*To you all flesh will come*
*with its burden of sin.*
*Too heavy for us, our offenses,*
*but you wipe them away.*

*Blessed is he whom you choose and call*
*to dwell in your courts.*
*We are filled with the blessings of your house,*
*of your holy temple.*

*You keep your pledge with wonders,*
*O God our savior,*
*the hope of all the earth*
*and of far distant isles.*

*You uphold the mountains with your strength,*
*you are girded with power.*
*You still the roaring of the seas,*
*the roaring of their waves*
*and the tumult of the peoples.*

*The ends of the earth stand in awe*
*at the sight of your wonders.*
*The lands of sunrise and sunset*
*you fill with your joy.*

*You care for the earth, give it water,*
*you fill it with riches.*
*Your river in heaven brims over*
*to provide its grain.*

*And thus you provide for the earth;*
*you drench its furrows,*
*you level it, soften it with showers,*
*you bless its growth.*

*You crown the year with your goodness.*
*Abundance flows in your steps,*
*in the pastures of the wilderness it flows.*

*The hills are girded with joy,*
*the meadows covered with flocks,*
*the valleys are decked with wheat.*
*They shout for joy, yes, they sing.*

**Reflections.** This psalm recalls only a few of the many dimensions of God's creative and providential love. As we contemplate his blessings, a spirit of genuine gratitude fills our hearts.

"To you we pay our vows," is the fulfillment of a pledge which the Hebrews made to God. When they petitioned God for some favor or blessing, they would promise him something in return. Fulfilling this "vow" was an expression of gratitude.

"To you all flesh will come with its burden of sin" is an acknowledgment that God alone can forgive sin. Redemption is God's greatest gift to us. It is really the gift of himself in the person of Jesus. Forgiveness is one of the many facets of God's merciful compassion. His love remains ever fathomless and mysterious.

When we repent, we open ourselves to the presence of God dwelling within us. God's loving mercy brings us to a greater appreciation of his divine indwelling. "Blessed is he whom you choose and call."

The "mountains" and the "seas" are symbols of the power and might of God. These are beyond man's control; hence, in our helplessness we recognize God's immensity.

"The lands of sunrise and sunset you fill with joy" is an expression of God's loving care. It helps us to visualize God as the source of life throughout the world. It also speaks to us of God's enduring love which never leaves us day or night.

"You care for the earth, give it water" expresses the gratitude of a person who lives in an arid country and who can fully appreciate the river in heaven brimming over.

The psalmist recognizes that the spring rains,

the heat of the harvest sun, and the fertility of the land are all blessings from a provident Father. How beautifully the writer expresses this recognition of God's goodness: "You crown the year with your goodness. / Abundance flows in your steps."

Overwhelmed by the graciousness of God, the psalmist wants to tell the Lord that all creation is delighted with his goodness: "The hills are girded with joy. / They shout for joy, yes, they sing."

**The Life of Jesus.** Jesus set an example for us in showing his own gratitude. On numerous occasions the gospel says simply, "He gave thanks."

Jesus taught us a powerful lesson about the importance of gratitude. When he cured the ten lepers, only one returned to praise and thank him. Jesus' memorable words reflect his disappointment: "Were not all ten made whole? Where are the other nine? Was there no one to return and give thanks to God except this foreigner?" (Lk 17:11ff).

St. Paul assures us that God responds to our prayer when it is offered with a grateful heart: "Present your needs to God in every form of prayer and in petitions full of gratitude" (Phil 4:6).

**The Life of the Church.** Every year we celebrate

Thanksgiving Day to remind us of the debt we owe to a provident Father who supplies all our temporal and spiritual needs.

Our annual celebration serves also as a reminder that every day must be a "thanksgiving day." Each day, and many times throughout the day, we need to pause to express our gratitude to God.

The Father loves a grateful heart. He responds to our expressions of appreciation with an even greater outpouring of his gifts. God not only created our world, but he continues to nourish and energize our land, empowering it to produce a rich harvest.

As we enjoy a good meal, we can contemplate God's goodness in providing the seed, the climatic conditions, the people who planted, nurtured, harvested, transported, and prepared the food for us.

Furthermore, it is God through his almighty power that brings new life and new color after the death of winter by providing the rains and the sunshine essential for a rich harvest.

What a joy to know that the same power which raised Jesus from the dead will also raise us from the dead after we have worked through the winter of life.

For all this, let us praise and thank our loving Father with all the joy of our hearts.

## Psalm 100
### A Joyous Heart Sings

Christians are naturally a joyous people. Followers of Jesus are persons who experience within themselves genuine Christian joy.

Likewise Christians must always be a grateful people.

In this short hymn of joy and thanksgiving the psalmist bids us to: "Cry out with joy to the Lord," "Serve the Lord with gladness," and "Come before him, singing for joy."

This short hymn was probably sung as the worshipers entered the Temple. We, like them, can sing joyfully and gratefully as we enter into our spiritual temple, the temple of our hearts, the inner sanctum where we meet the Lord in prayer.

With joy let us pray:

*Cry out with joy to the Lord, all the earth.*
*Serve the Lord with gladness.*
*Come before him, singing for joy.*

*Know that he, the Lord, is God.*
*He made us, we belong to him,*
*we are his people, the sheep of his flock.*

*Go within his gates, giving thanks.*
*Enter his courts with songs of praise.*
*Give thanks to him and bless his name.*

*Indeed, how good is the Lord,*
*eternal his merciful love.*
*He is faithful from age to age.*

**Reflections.** The psalmist invites us to sing for joy because we belong to the Lord in a very special way. His repetition emphasizes our special prerogative: "He made us, we belong to him, / we are his people, the sheep of his flock."

This awareness of belonging to the Lord fills the psalmist's heart with gladness and gratitude. He knows how much God loves those he created. This realization leads the psalmist into an outburst of gratitude.

His conclusion, then, is a doxology of praise: "Indeed, how good is the Lord/ eternal his merciful love. / He is faithful from age to age."

**The Life of Jesus.** This invitation to sing joyfully to the Lord is reiterated many times in our Christian life. Who can have a greater reason to be joyous than redeemed Christians who have experienced God's love.

Jesus himself revealed the reason why we should be a happy, joyous people. He told us the good news of salvation. Nothing can rob us of the joy of heaven; hence joy should permeate our days here on earth: "All this I tell you that my joy may be yours and your joy may be complete" (Jn 15:11).

We belong to our loving Father. The Father not only created us, but he also gave us his Son as our Savior and Redeemer. Jesus explains to us why he came into the world: "I came that they might have life / and have it to the full" (Jn 10:10).

In the same breath, he tells us how he will accomplish our redemption: "The Father loves me for this: / that I lay down my life / to take it up again. / No one takes it from me; / I lay it down freely" (Jn 10:17f).

What greater cause of joy could we have?

I once commented to a Christian in Israel that the Jews as a whole did not seem to be a happy people. His answer was immediate: "They do not know that they are redeemed."

**The Life of the Church.** In the Liturgy of the Word on Thursday of the eighth week in ordinary time, the church joins together the words of St. Peter and the account of the healing of Bartimaeus with this psalm of joy.

Peter reminds us that we should be a happy people because we are "a chosen race, a royal priesthood, a consecrated nation, a people he claims for his own" (1 Pt 2:9).

In the good news, we see Jesus touching blind Bartimaeus with his healing power restoring his sight. "Immediately he received his sight and started to follow him up the road" (Mk 10:46f).

As the eyes of our faith are opened, we can grasp more fully the Lord's boundless goodness to us. Then will our hearts abound with joy.

In this Liturgy of the Word, Psalm 100 is an ideal response to these two scriptures.

St. Paul gives an additional reason for our joy: "You have been purchased, and at a price! So glorify God in your body" (1 Cor 6:20).

To this we add the words of St. Peter: "Realize that you were delivered from the futile way of life your fathers handed on to you, not by any diminishable sum of silver or gold, but by Christ's blood beyond all price: the blood of a spotless unblemished lamb" (1 Pt 1:18ff).

Pondering these words of St. Peter and St. Paul may fill our hearts with sorrow, but it will be a sorrow mingled generously with joy. Then our hearts will sing anew this psalm of joy.

# EIGHT

# Home

## Psalm 127
### Vestibule of Heaven

OUR HOMES ARE BEING BOMBARDED with all kinds of materialistic and humanistic philosophies. Television, radio, and telephones have invaded the privacy of our family life. Pressures of every description are brought to bear upon us, threatening the comfort and peace which God intends in family life.

Happiness is falsely portrayed as self-gratification, seeking pleasures which will never satisfy the longing of the human heart.

God intends our homes to be havens of peace and joy; oases where we experience loving care and concern. The psalmist knew that only when God was the center of family life, would we achieve all the blessings he intends.

In this prayer, the psalmist expresses his trust in God. He reminds us that undue anxiety and worry are an insult to God. With the people of the

Old Testament, he realizes the necessity of total dependence upon God.

Without God's blessing, all human activity is futile. The writer prays for food, family, and dwelling, which come from God. He realizes, too, that success and contentment depend upon God's blessing.

The psalmist had the same concerns about home and family which we have. He turned to the Lord with this powerful prayer. Let us join him.

*If the Lord does not build the house,*
*in vain do its builders labor;*
*if the Lord does not watch over the city,*
*in vain does the watchman keep vigil.*

*In vain is your earlier rising,*
*your going later to rest,*
*you who toil for the bread you eat:*
*when he pours gifts on his beloved while they*
*   slumber.*

*Truly sons are a gift from the Lord,*
*a blessing, the fruit of the womb.*
*Indeed the sons of youth*
*are like arrows in the hand of a warrior.*

*O the happiness of the man*
*who has filled his quiver with these arrows!*
*He will have no cause for shame*
*when he disputes with his foes in the gateways.*

**Reflections.** "If the Lord does not build the house, / in vain do its builders labor. . . ." Building a house also means founding a family. God is the author of family life and the source of its blessings.

"In vain is your earlier rising, . . ." This verse is also a reminder that without God's blessings all human endeavors are fruitless. God gives the increase. God's gifts are freely given if they are accepted. This is what the psalmist means when he says: "He pours gifts on his beloved while they slumber."

"Truly sons are a gift from the Lord, . . ." The Hebrews recognized that God alone is the giver of life. The greatest possession a Hebrew could have was a large family. Sterility was considered a curse from God. " . . . who has filled his quiver with these arrows." This expression is a metaphoric way of recounting the blessings of a large family. The "quiver" is the home and the "arrows" are children.

According to a custom of that day, the larger the family the greater the influence of the father in the local government at the city gates. "He will have no cause for shame / when he disputes with his foes in the gateways."

**The Life of Jesus.** There are many exhortations in the Old Testament to trust in the Lord. The New Testament issues an even stronger appeal for total trust in the goodness of God. Jesus pleaded with us to trust in the Father. In the Sermon on the Mount, he points out to us how God cares for the birds in the sky and lilies of the field. Then he assures us that the Father's concern for us is far greater: "Your heavenly Father knows all that you need. Seek first his kingship over you, his way of holiness, and all these things will be given you besides" (Mt 6:25ff).

On another occasion, Jesus gave us an excellent example of how much we need to depend on God and how little we can do ourselves. He explained how the reign of God could grow and develop in a household: "A man scatters seed on the ground. He goes to bed and gets up day after day. Through it all the seed sprouts and grows without his knowing how it happens. The soil produces of itself the first blade, then the ear, finally the ripe wheat in the ear" (Mk 4:26ff).

The divine life which God gives us does the same in our hearts. If permitted to develop, it draws us into a deeper union with him and with others, particularly the members of our family.

Jesus reminds us: "Apart from me you can do nothing" (Jn 15:5).

Jesus informed us of the conditions necessary for the divine presence to be dynamic and operative within us and our family: "Anyone who loves me will be true to my word, / and my Father will love him; / we will come to him and make our dwelling place with him" (Jn 14:23).

May our home and every home truly become his dwelling place.

**The Life of the Church.** In our Christian liturgy we bring the Lord to an unbaptized person so that the Lord may build his home within that person. In Baptism, we become temples of the Holy Spirit:

> You are the temple of the living God, just as God said: 'I will dwell with them and walk among them. I will be their God and they shall be my people. . . . I will welcome you and be a father to you and you will be my sons and daughters.'
>
> (2 Cor 6:16; see also 1 Cor 3:16, 6:19)

In his pastoral zeal, St. Paul reminds us that he is a co-worker, but we are God's building: "We are God's co-workers, while you are his cultivation, his building" (1 Cor 3:9).

He then reminds us that we can build on this foundation with gold, silver, precious stones, wood, hay, or straw. But "fire" will test the quality of each man's work.

As Christians, we can think of the divine presence of the Holy Spirit as the home he is building within us. The arrows in our quiver, then, are the gifts and fruits with which he fills us:

"O the happiness of the man / who has filled his quiver with these arrows."

## *Psalm 128*
## *A Bit of Heaven*

Psalm 128 provides a natural sequence to the previous psalm. In Psalm 127 we prayed for the Lord's blessings of happiness and love, peace and prosperity for our own family. In this psalm, we turn our attention to other families. We pray the same blessings for them.

As God blesses each family, they, in turn, will begin to form a peaceful, God-fearing community "in a happy Jerusalem."

The psalmist rejoices with the man whom God has blessed with a loving wife and healthy children. He asks for prosperity and long life. It was a common belief among the Hebrews that any man who lived according to God's law would be blessed with a devoted wife and good children.

The inspired writer also asks for a "happy Jerusalem," which will be made up of many happy families. Each family is a part of the community and will contribute to the spiritual well-being of the whole community.

With the words of the psalmist, let us pray for happiness and peace in our own family so that we can help form a "happy Jerusalem."

*O blessed are those who fear the Lord*
*and walk in his ways!*

*By the labor of your hands you shall eat.*
*You will be happy and prosper;*
*your wife like a fruitful vine*
*in the heart of your house:*
*your children like shoots of the olive,*
*around your table.*

*Indeed thus shall be blessed*
*the man who fears the Lord.*
*May the Lord bless you from Zion*
*all the days of your life!*
*May you see your children's children*
*in a happy Jerusalem!*

*On Israel, peace!*

**Reflections.** In poetic imagery the author tries to describe the ideal family: "Your wife like a fruitful vine ... / your children like shoots of the olive. ..."

The people of the Old Testament lived close to nature. The inspired writers of the Old Testament often used metaphors to illustrate the blessings of the Lord to those who loved him: "The just man shall flourish like a palm tree / like a cedar of Lebanon shall he grow" (Ps 92:3).

In figurative language and at great length, the

author of the Book of Proverbs tries to describe the ideal wife. After extolling her many virtues, he points to the love which her husband and children have for her. This will testify to her goodness and dedication: "Her children rise up and praise her; / her husband, too, extols her" (Prv 31:10ff).

**The Life of Jesus.** The home of the holy family in Nazareth is hallowed as the ideal home. It was a house of prayer. Jesus sanctified it by his presence. An atmosphere of love, dedication, solitude, and prayer prevailed throughout.

Jesus' family prayed. They observed the ritual and prayers of their people. They went to the Temple and to the synagogue as was their custom.

After Jesus was lost in the Temple at the age of twelve, the evangelist narrates the sequel in these words:

> He [Jesus] went down with them then, and came to Nazareth and was obedient to them. His mother meanwhile kept all these things in memory. Jesus, for his part, progressed steadily in wisdom and age and grace before God and men (Lk 2:51f).

After his triumphal entry into Jerusalem, Jesus drove the money-changers and the dove-sellers from the Temple, reminding them of the words of scripture: "My house shall be called a house of prayer, but you are turning it into a den of thieves" (Mt 21:12ff).

Should we not be equally zealous in eradicating all the pernicious influences which threaten the peace and joy of our own family, as well as our extended family?

Truly, then, our home will become a house of prayer and the vestibule of heaven.

**The Life of the Church.** St. Paul gives some pastoral directives which encompass both the natural family and the ecclesial family:

> Husbands, love your wives, as Christ loved the Church. . . . This is a great foreshadowing. I mean it refers to Christ and the Church. In any case, each one should love his wife as he loves himself, the wife for her part showing respect for her husband (Eph 5:25, 32).

The liturgy also speaks of the ideal spiritual home. The "new Jerusalem" is made up of all Christian families united spiritually as the people of God. Jesus invites us to eat "at the table of the Lord" in order to form a special community—the family of God.

Again it is St. Paul who asks an important rhetorical question: "And is not the bread we break a sharing in the body of Christ? Because the loaf of bread is one, we, many though we are, are one body, for we partake of the one loaf" (1 Cor 10:16).

As the psalmist prayed fervently for a "happy Jerusalem," we, too, should pray for a renewed and happy Jerusalem. Then will our home become a little church nurturing the spiritual and physical life of the whole family.

## Psalm 113
### Joyful Mother

To pray Psalm 113 sincerely, we need to examine various areas of our life. Are we happy with our station in life? Do we envy those who seem to be more gifted or more talented than we are? Do we feel inadequate to cope with the diverse problems which arise daily? Do we recognize our own inability to accomplish what is expected of us?

If we feel that we fall into one or other of these categories, then we have the proper frame of mind to praise God in the words of the psalmist.

This hymn is an invitation to everyone to praise the Lord, especially for his loving concern for the lowly. The lowly are those the world regards as unimportant. They are the unlettered, the poor, and the downtrodden. The world usually shuns these people and often despises them.

The lowly are those, too, who recognize that by

themselves they can do nothing. They are willing to turn to God to seek his help and guidance in daily living.

The psalmist summons us to praise the Lord for his tender love for the lowly.

> *Praise, O servants of the Lord,*
> *praise the name of the Lord!*
> *May the name of the Lord be blessed*
> *both now and for evermore!*
> *From the rising of the sun to its setting*
> *praised be the name of the Lord!*
>
> *High above all the nations is the Lord,*
> *above the heavens his glory.*
> *Who is like the Lord, our God,*
> *who has risen on high to his throne*
> *yet stoops from the heights to look down,*
> *to look down upon heaven and earth?*
>
> *From the dust he lifts up the lowly,*
> *from his misery he raises the poor*
> *to set him in the company of princes,*
> *yes, with the princes of his people.*
> *To the childless wife he gives a home*
> *and gladdens her heart with children.*

**Reflections.** "Praise, O servants of the Lord, / praise the name of the Lord!" The psalmist knows that only the humble and righteous are able to understand God's greatness and sound his praises from their hearts. The proud find it difficult to praise God joyously because they do not appreciate his tremendous outpouring of love.

"From the rising of the sun to its setting / praised be the name of the Lord!" This expression means all day long from morning until evening. It also means from east to west, thus including everyone everywhere. Praise should arise at all times and in all places to our compassionate Father.

In this prayer, we recognize that the God of might and power, the God who created the universe and maintains order in it, is concerned for and loves the lowly. "From the dust he lifts up the lowly, / from his misery he raises the poor. . . ."

In the psalmist's day, a barren woman was considered disgraced and cursed by God. In this psalm, we praise God for reaching out tenderly to the childless wife: "To the childless wife he gives a home / and gladdens her heart with children."

**The Life of Jesus.** In her magnificent song of praise, our Blessed Mother recalls God's favor to the lowly: "For he has looked upon his servant in her lowliness; all ages to come shall call me blessed. God who is mighty has done great things for me, holy is his name" (Lk 1:48).

Jesus himself was lowly. He came from a

carpenter's family. He was not trained in the rabbinical schools. He came from the backward village of Nazareth.

Jesus proclaimed a special beatitude for the lowly: "Blest are the lowly; they shall inherit the land" (Mt 5:5).

Jesus also invited us to come to him to learn lowliness: "Learn from me, for I am gentle and humble of heart" (Mt 11:29).

How clearly Jesus pronounced the fate of the proud and the reward of the humble: "The greatest among you will be the one who serves the rest. Whoever exalts himself shall be humbled, but whoever humbles himself shall be exalted" (Mt 23:11f).

**The Life of the Church.** The church has always extolled the humility and the lowliness of the saints. Spiritual writers throughout the centuries have emphasized the necessity of humility. Perhaps none has expressed it as simply and as pointedly as did St. Ignatius. He outlined three kinds of humility.

The first kind is necessary for salvation. It requires the willingness to subject and humble ourselves in order to obey the law of God in all things.

The second engenders in us a spirit of indifference, so that we desire riches no more than poverty, honor no more than dishonor, a long life no more than a short life. All this we seek according to God's will for us.

The third is most perfect and presumes that we have already attained the first two. It consist in this: that we desire and choose poverty with Christ rather than riches; insults with Christ rather than honors; to be accounted as a fool for Christ rather than considered wise in the world. Since Jesus was treated in this way, we will be more like him.

"Learn from me, for I am gentle and humble of heart" (Mt 11:29).

# NINE

# God Is Trustworthy

## Psalm 62
### Unshakeable Confidence

A DISQUIETING FACTOR which often insinuates itself into our daily lives is a lack of confidence and trust, sometimes in ourselves, more frequently in others, and even in God. This lack of trust can easily progress from a simple doubt to a paralyzing fear, from an ordinary worry to a growing anxiety.

In Psalm 62, the psalmist recalls the reasons for his well-founded confidence and trust in God alone.

God is called "Rock" repeatedly in the Old Testament, especially in the psalms. God is truly a "rock" of strength and a solid foundation upon which we can build all our hopes and expectations.

The Israelites were familiar with the strength of rock. Their fields and vineyards were planted in irregular shapes, determined, to a great extent, by the many outcroppings of rock over the landscape. Their most common building material was cut stone.

The image of the Lord as rock is certainly comforting and consoling.

With the expectant faith of the psalmist let us pray:

*In God alone is my soul at rest;*
*my help comes from him.*
*He alone is my rock, my stronghold,*
*my fortress: I stand firm.*

*How long will you all attack one man*
*to break him down,*
*as though he were a tottering wall,*
*or a tumbling fence?*

*Their plan is only to destroy:*
*they take pleasure in lies.*
*With their mouth they utter blessing*
*but in their heart they curse.*

*In God alone be at rest, my soul;*
*for my hope comes from him.*
*He alone is my rock, my stronghold,*
*my fortress: I stand firm.*

*In God is my safety and glory,*
*the rock of my strength.*

*Take refuge in God, all you people.*
*Trust him at all times.*
*Pour out your hearts before him*
*for God is our refuge.*

*Common folk are only a breath,*
*great men an illusion.*
*Placed in the scales, they rise;*
*they weigh less than a breath.*

*Do not put your trust in oppression*
*nor vain hopes on plunder.*
*Do not set your heart on riches*
*even when they increase.*

*For God has said only one thing:*
*only two do I know:*
*that to God alone belongs power*
*and to you, Lord, love;*
*and that you repay each man*
*according to his deeds.*

**Reflections.** The psalmist does not make a frenzied appeal for help. He has the calm assurance of a man who trusts that God will take care of everything.

"In God alone is my soul at rest." These words are an affirmation of trust in God, despite the threats and dangers the psalmist faces. Like the psalmist, we need to verbalize our trust in God in order to strengthen it within ourselves.

The psalmist repeats words such as "alone" and "only" to reaffirm that he can place all his hope and trust in God.

"How long will you attack one man? . . ." The author addresses his enemies but has no fear of their lying lips and curses, because God is his Rock. With graphic language he assures them that he is not a "tottering wall or tumbling fence."

The psalmist has so much confidence in God that he reaches out to all his own people and exhorts them to place their trust in God's love. He is hoping that his earnest plea will reach our ears also. "Take refuge in God, all you people. / Trust in him at all times. . . ."

In direct contrast to God as rock is the illusory and inadequate help of human beings. Human solutions are neither infallible nor trustworthy. "Common folk are only a breath, / great men an illusion. . . ."

God is not only a God of might and power, but he is also a God of infinite love. His boundless love impels him to come to our assistance when we need him. "To God alone belongs power / and to you, Lord, love."

**The Life of Jesus.** In the Sermon on the Mount, Jesus paints a reassuring picture of the provident love of the Father. He, too, uses the illustration of solid rock. Jesus assures us that the wise man does not build his house on sand, where the winds and floods can destroy it. The wise man builds his house on solid rock. Jesus reinforces the point of the psalmist. (Mt 7:24ff)

Again and again, Jesus reassures us and asks us to trust his Father and himself as well: "Do not let your hearts be troubled. / Have faith in God and faith in me" (Jn 14:1).

Again he implores us to trust him: "Fear is useless. What is needed is trust." (Mk 5:36)

Listen to the tenderness of Jesus when he says, "Do not live in fear, little flock. It has pleased your Father to give you the kingdom" (Lk 12:32).

Such expressions as "Fear not" and "Don't be afraid" are used three hundred times in scriptures. The Lord wants to remind us continually of his care and concern for each one of us.

**The Life of the Church.** The calm reassurance with which this psalm fills our hearts is also reiterated in the Liturgy of the Word at Mass and in the Liturgy of the Hours.

The readings selected for the Eucharistic Celebration renew and strengthen our confidence and trust in our loving Father, since it is Jesus himself who speaks to us through his word.

In giving pastoral advice and guidance to

Timothy, St. Paul is also speaking to us: "Tell those who are rich in this world's goods not to be proud, and not to rely on so uncertain a thing as wealth. Let them trust in the God who provides us richly with all things for our use" (1 Tm 6:17).

Let us pray for ourselves and with one another. "So may God, the source of all hope, fill you with all joy and peace in believing so that through the power of the Holy Spirit you may hope in abundance" (Rom 15:13).

## Psalm 16
### Trust in God Brings True Happiness

The psalmist is confident that his loyalty to the Lord and his avoidance of those who refuse to worship the one true God will be the source of his happiness.

It is easy to give the Lord lip service while we permit the tin gods of self-centeredness and pride or pleasure and self-gratification to take over in our lives. Experience teaches us that these pursuits are unsatisfying. We soon discover that these tin gods lead us only to regret and disillusionment and leave our hearts empty.

Perhaps this experience is necessary. It may lead us back to a deeper, more personal relationship with our loving Father. As we begin to relate to him more deeply, he gives us an even greater desire to trust him.

This psalm assures us that as we give our loyal service to God, we will be certain that his love will never leave us, but will lead us to our eternal home with him.

Let us make the psalmist's words our own as we pray with him.

*Preserve me, O God, I take refuge in you.*
*I say to the Lord: "You are my God.*
*My happiness lies in you alone."*

*He has put into my heart a marvellous love*
*for the faithful ones who dwell in his land.*
*Those who choose other gods increase their sorrows.*
*Never will I offer their offerings of blood.*
*Never will I take their name upon my lips.*

*O Lord, it is you who are my portion and cup;*
*it is you yourself who are my prize.*
*The lot marked out for me is my delight:*
*welcome indeed the heritage that falls to me!*

*I will bless the Lord who gives me counsel,*
*who even at night directs my heart.*
*I keep the Lord ever in my sight:*
*since he is at my right hand, I shall stand firm.*

*And so my heart rejoices, my soul is glad;*
*even my body shall rest in safety.*
*For you will not leave my soul among the dead,*

*nor let your beloved know decay.*

*You will show me the path of life,*
*the fullness of joy in your presence,*
*at your right hand happiness for ever.*

**Reflections.** The psalmist sets forth his first and foremost priority in life as he prays, "I say to the Lord: 'You are my God. / My happiness lies in you alone.'"

For us, too, God is our final end in life. As we pursue that end, we will discover peace and happiness. Any deviation will lead us to misery and desolation.

"He has put into my heart a marvellous love / for the faithful ones who dwell in his land." We are among those "faithful ones." As we grow in our appreciation of our adoption as sons and daughters of the Father, we will realize how closely we are united with the whole heavenly court—the angels and saints as well as our own deceased loved ones. What better expression can we have than the words of the psalmist. What greater incentive to bring us into a genuine trust.

This realization draws us further away from those "who choose other gods." These "gods" may creep into our lives unwittingly. For some of us, it may be our strong will, our pride, our self-interests. These can be the false gods in our lives.

Once again the psalmist declares his priority:

"O Lord, it is you who are my portion and cup."

If the Lord is our "portion and cup," then we begin to appreciate how important we are to him. What greater "prize" could we attain than "the heritage that falls to me."

In verses 8 to 10, the psalmist proves himself a real mystic. He foresees his own resurrection as his heritage from the Lord. His contemplative prayer gave him insights beyond human knowledge. We know of our own resurrection through revelation and the promise of Jesus.

Finally the psalmist is assured that the Lord will show him the way of life: "The fullness of joy in your presence / at your right hand happiness for ever."

**The Life of Jesus.** Jesus came into the world to proclaim the good news and also to map out the path we are to follow: "I am the way, and the truth, and the life" (Jn 14:6).

He also assured us, "I am the light of the world. / No follower of mine shall ever walk in darkness; / no, he shall possess the light of life" (Jn 8:12).

This was all made possible because Jesus took on our human nature that he might redeem it. One of the principal fruits of the redemption is the capacity given us to receive his divine life. We are able to receive it partially now, but in full measure when we reach our eternal home with him. Jesus stated this truth in these words:

> I am the resurrection and the life; / whoever believes in me, / though he should die, will come to life; / and whoever is alive and believes in me / will never die (Jn 11:25).

What greater source of happiness and trust could we expect than this assurance from Jesus. Jesus not only promised us eternal life, but he continues to pray that we accept it: "Father, all those you gave me I would have in my company, where I am to see this glory of mine" (Jn 17:24).

**The Life of the Church.** Throughout scripture we are admonished repeatedly to trust and not to be fearful; to hope and have confidence. Jesus took up the same refrain, constantly reminding us not to be afraid, but to trust.

> Fear is useless. What is needed is trust.
> (Mk 5:36)

> Fear nothing, then. You are worth more than a flock of sparrows (Lk 12:7).

> Do not live in fear, little flock. It has pleased your Father to give you the kingdom.
> (Lk 12:32)

> I say to you who are my friends: do not be

afraid of those who kill the body and can do no more (Lk 12:4).

Get hold of yourselves! It is I. Do not be afraid! (Mt 14:27)

These are but a few of the many times Jesus advised us to trust and not fear.

As we appreciate more and more how much the Lord loves us, and as we try to respond to his love, fear will become more remote in our lives.

The Apostle John sums it all up in a few words: "Love has no room for fear; / rather, perfect love casts out all fear" (1 Jn 4:18).

## Psalm 146
### In God We Trust

The Founding Fathers of the United States showed great wisdom when they decided that our currency should bear the inscription, "In God We Trust."

Each day as coins pass through our hands we are reminded that our complete trust in God will bring us true happiness. The psalms likewise keep this truth before us. Numerous psalms have as their central theme trust in God.

Psalm 146 is the first in the final series of five *hallel* psalms which end the psalter. These are all songs of praise. In Psalm 146, we praise God for all his faithfulness in caring for us.

This psalm is a simple hymn extolling the power and the goodness of the Lord. In order to focus our attention and increase our trust in God, the psalmist contrasts the frailty and unfaithfulness of man with the fidelity of God.

A sign in a little shop bespeaks the same truth: "In God We Trust—Others Pay Cash."

As we pray with the psalmist, our trust in our Lord will be strengthened; therefore, let us pray:

*My soul, give praise to the Lord;*
*I will praise the Lord all my days,*
*make music to my God while I live.*

*Put no trust in princes,*
*in mortal men in whom there is no help.*
*Take their breath, they return to clay*
*and their plans that day come to nothing.*

*He is happy who is helped by Jacob's God,*
*whose hope is in the Lord his God,*
*who alone made heaven and earth,*
*the seas and all they contain.*

*It is he who keeps faith for ever,*
*who is just to those who are oppressed.*
*It is he who gives bread to the hungry,*
*the Lord, who sets prisoners free,*

*the Lord who gives sight to the blind,*

*who raises up those who are bowed down,*
*the Lord, who protects the stranger*
*and upholds the widow and orphan.*

*It is the Lord who loves the just*
*but thwarts the path of the wicked.*
*The Lord will reign for ever,*
*Zion's God, from age to age.*

**Reflections.** "My soul, give praise to the Lord."
Even though these words are spoken to himself,
the author invites us to join him in praising God
because he is faithful and trustworthy.

"Put no trust in princes" can be understood in
two ways. First, it refers to the powerful and rich
leaders. Second, it embraces all human beings.
These mortals cannot help us in most areas of our
life. The psalmist makes this plea because he
knows that the average person would more
willingly put trust in other people than in God.

"He is happy . . . whose hope is in the Lord his
God." True happiness comes from the humility
necessary for trusting God and also from the
experience of God's faithfulness to his promises.

"It is he who gives bread to the hungry. . . ." The
psalmist lists these divine attributes as a means of
setting forth reasons why we should place im-
plicit trust and confidence in God.

And finally: "The Lord will reign for ever."

**The Life of Jesus.** Mary perfectly fulfilled the role of a disciple of Jesus. From the first moment of her call, she placed her trust in God's word.

At the time of the Annunciation, she needed unfailing trust in God. The moment she whispered her fiat, the Word became flesh. No such conception had ever taken place, yet Mary believed. She trusted that God would effect his will in her.

When she went in haste into the hill country to visit Elizabeth, her cousin acknowledged Mary's great trust: "Blest is she who trusted that the Lord's words to her would be fulfilled" (Lk 1:45).

Mary's journey to Bethlehem, her escape into the sanctuary of Egypt, her heart-rending climb to Calvary, and her loneliness after the Ascension were all journeys in faith and trust.

Mary is a model of genuine trust and confidence. Jesus himself attested to this fact. When a woman in the crowd complimented his Mother, Jesus called attention to her true greatness: "Rather, blest are they who hear the word of God and keep it" (Lk 11:28).

With a listening heart, Mary heard that word and because she trusted, she was able to keep it.

**The Life of the Church.** One of the reasons for Mary's uncompromising trust in God was the fact that she knew of God's fidelity to her people. Mary prayed the psalms fervently with her people. The psalms form a record of the Israelites' experience of God in their history.

In her prayer, Mary experienced God's love. She saw how God had provided for and guided his people. She understood the trust which her people long ago placed in God. Her own trust must have increased immensely as she pondered the wonders of God's love.

Jesus taught us to trust in the powerful intercessory prayer of his Mother. At the wedding feast in Cana, Jesus responded to the request of his Mother even though his hour had not yet come.

We, too, have confidence in the power of her prayer as we daily say, "Pray for us sinners now and at the hour of our death."

Let us often pray: "Remember, O most gracious Virgin Mary, that never was it known that anyone who fled to your protection, implored your help, or sought your intercession was left unaided. Inspired by this confidence, I fly unto you, O Virgin of virgins, my Mother. To you do I come, before you I stand sinful and sorrowful. O Mother of the Word Incarnate, despise not my petitions but in your mercy hear and answer me. Amen."

TEN

# Full Orchestra of Praise

*Psalm 98*
*In Praise of Our Victorious King*

PARENTS OF AN INFANT anxiously await the first sounds their child will utter. They treasure those sounds and encourage the child to form intelligible words.

As the child grows, he becomes capable of expressing some words of thanks and praise to his parents for all they have done. The parents, in turn, are delighted by such expressions. This gives us a faint insight into the reaction of our heavenly Father when his children strive to express their heartfelt praise and thanks to him.

In Psalm 98, we hail God as our victorious King. He has conquered sin and opened the way to salvation for all his people. The psalmist invites us to praise God especially for his gift of salvation. We are encouraged to praise him with a new

153

song. This could mean that we are to continue to sing our song of praise with greater fervor or with a deeper sense of appreciation for his marvelous work of our redemption.

May our sincerity give a new lilt to our song of praise as we join the psalmist.

*Sing a new song to the Lord*
*for he has worked wonders.*
*His right hand and his holy arm*
*have brought salvation.*

*The Lord has made known his salvation;*
*has shown his justice to the nations.*
*He has remembered his truth and love*
*for the house of Israel.*

*All the ends of the earth have seen*
*the salvation of our God.*
*Shout to the Lord, all the earth,*
*ring out your joy.*

*Sing psalms to the Lord with the harp,*
*with the sound of music.*
*With trumpets and the sound of the horn*
*acclaim the King, the Lord.*

*Let the sea and all within it thunder;*
*the world, and all its peoples.*
*Let the rivers clap their hands*
*and the hills ring out their joy.*

*Rejoice at the presence of the Lord,*
*for he comes to rule the earth.*
*He will rule the world with justice*
*and the peoples with fairness.*

**Reflections.** "Sing a new song" is an invitation to praise God because "His right hand and his holy arm / have brought salvation."

The second section of the psalm extends a universal invitation to praise God because "All the ends of the earth have seen / the salvation of our God."

The psalmist wants the praise of God to be harmoniously orchestrated with harp, trumpets, and the sound of the horn. "Sing psalms to the Lord with the harp / with the sound of music. / With trumpets, and the sound of the horn / acclaim the King, the Lord."

The universality of the invitation to praise God is again emphasized when the psalmist calls upon nature—the sea, the rivers, and the hills to ring out their joy.

Nor does the psalmist want the praise of God to be subdued in any way: "Shout to the Lord, all the earth, / ring out your joy."

The inspired writer's final plea to us is: "Rejoice at the presence of the Lord."

**The Life of Jesus.** Jesus encouraged us to praise

his Father. We immediately recall the incident when Jesus himself paused to offer praise to the Father: "Father, Lord of heaven and earth, to you I offer praise; for what you have hidden from the learned and the clever you have revealed to the merest children" (Mt 11:25).

On numerous occasions the works of Jesus caused the onlookers to praise and glorify God. When he healed the paralytic at Capernaum, the crowd was deeply moved. "They were awestruck; all gave praise to God, saying, 'We have never seen anything like this!'" (Mk 2:12).

When Jesus healed the blind man on the road to Jericho, both the blind man and the crowd praised God. "At that very moment he was given his sight and began to follow him, giving God the glory. All the people witnessed it and they too gave praise to God" (Lk 18:43).

Jesus not only accepted, but also justified the praise he received on his triumphal entry into Jerusalem on Palm Sunday.

"Hosanna to the Son of David! / Blessed is he who comes in the name of the Lord! / Hosanna in the highest!" ... The chief priests and the scribes became indignant when they observed the wonders he worked, and how the children were shouting out in the temple precincts, "Hosanna to the Son of David!" "Do you hear what they are saying?" they asked him. Jesus said to them, "Of course I do! Did you never read this: 'From the speech of infants and children you have framed a hymn of praise?'" (Mt 21:9, and 15f).

**The Life of the Church.** The work of our redemption has been accomplished. Jesus founded his kingdom, his reign on earth. Nevertheless, we continue to pray, "Thy kingdom come." We still pray that all peoples will be open to receive the fruits of the redemption and that salvation may be perfected throughout the world. We pray that God's kingdom may come as more and more people respond to his saving power.

While praying this psalm, we look to the future when the Lord will come again. We await his final coming, when he will take possession of his kingdom and take us to our eternal home with him.

In preparation for his coming, we continue to sing his praises. In praising him, we recognize our own inadequacy and our total dependence upon him.

When praising him, we show our appreciation for the tremendous love which wrought our salvation. Our praise of God also helps us to die to our self so that the image of Jesus may be formed in us and so that we may "put on the new man" (Eph 4:23).

St. Paul tells us how to reach this goal: "Be

intent on the things above rather than on things on earth. After all, you have died! Your life is hidden now with Christ in God. When Christ our life appears, then you shall appear with him in glory" (Col 3:2ff).

We have every reason to "sing a new song to the Lord."

## Psalm 145
### A Great and Good God

The *hallel* psalms are magnificent prayers of praise extolling the majesty of God. They belong to every age and every people, but they are especially needed in our times.

Today commercial advertising dulls the meaning of praise. The media praises every product and person to a superlative degree — food and drink, soap and cosmetics, handy gadgets which should lighten work, people of questionable talent and character. Such advertising has rendered praise cheap and hollow.

The psalms of praise can do much to awaken within us the true meaning of praise by directing our attention to our loving Father, who alone is Holy, who alone is Lord.

These inspired hymns focus our praise and adoration on God, the Lord and Master of the universe. They bring us back to the real essence and purpose of praise.

The psalmist urges and encourages us to praise

God by calling our attention to his boundless love.

*I will give you glory, O God my King,*
*I will bless your name for ever.*

*I will bless you day after day*
*and praise your name for ever.*
*The Lord is great, highly to be praised,*
*his greatness cannot be measured.*

*Age to age shall proclaim your works,*
*shall declare your mighty deeds,*
*shall speak of your splendor and glory,*
*tell the tale of your wonderful works.*

*They will speak of your terrible deeds,*
*recount your greatness and might.*
*They will recall your abundant goodness;*
*age to age shall ring out your justice.*

*The Lord is kind and full of compassion,*
*slow to anger, abounding in love.*
*How good is the Lord to all,*
*compassionate to all his creatures.*

*All your creatures shall thank you, O Lord,*
*and your friends shall repeat their blessing.*
*They shall speak of the glory of your reign*
*and declare your might, O God,*

*to make known to men your mighty deeds*
*and the glorious splendor of your reign.*

*Yours is an everlasting kingdom;*
*your rule lasts from age to age.*

*The Lord is faithful in all his words*
*and loving in all his deeds.*
*The Lord supports all who fall*
*and raises all who are bowed down.*

*The eyes of all creatures look to you*
*and you give them their food in due time.*
*You open wide your hand,*
*grant the desires of all who live.*

*The Lord is just in all his ways*
*and loving in all his deeds.*
*He is close to all who call him,*
*who call on him from their hearts.*

*He grants the desires of those who fear him,*
*he hears their cry and he saves them.*
*The Lord protects all who love him;*
*but the wicked he will utterly destroy.*

*Let me speak the praise of the Lord,*
*let all mankind bless his holy name*
*for ever, for ages unending.*

**Reflections.** "I will give you glory, O God, my King." In the first person, the psalmist joyfully plunges into his hymn of praise, giving glory to God, blessing his name and praising his measureless greatness.

Next the psalmist wishes to praise God for his goodness. Words fail him as he tries to describe the providential love of God manifested in his "Mighty deeds and wonderful works." The "deeds and works" of God refer to his work of creation and his redemptive work which is the means of salvation to all.

"The Lord is kind and full of compassion"— these words stir us to greater gratitude for his loving forgiveness and his understanding of our human weaknesses.

"The Lord is faithful in all his words and loving in all his deeds." The goodness of the Lord is all-embracing. In order for us to adequately comprehend and appreciate his goodness, we must slowly and contemplatively pray this psalm again. Such a repetition will create a deeper sense of gratitude in our hearts.

After enumerating the goodness of the Lord, the psalmist renews his plea: "Let all mankind bless his holy name / for ever, for ages unending."

**The Life of Jesus.** In this psalm, as in most of the hymns found in the Psalter, the sacred writers praise the boundless providential love of the Lord. Jesus never failed to do the same.

Furthermore, Jesus manifested his own providential love for us. On the Mount of Beatitudes, Jesus used pastoral imagery to draw attention to the Father's love. "Look at the birds in the sky. They do not sow or reap, they gather nothing into barns; yet your heavenly Father feeds them. Are not you more important than they?" (Mt 6:26).

With love, Jesus performed "the first of his signs at Cana in Galilee" providing for the celebration of the wedding feast. (Jn 2:1ff)

Jesus did not disperse the hungry people who had listened to his teaching, but fed the entire crowd with "five barley loaves and a couple of dried fish." (Jn 6:1ff)

Jesus promised that whatever we ask the Father in his name would be granted to us. Daily reflection on this point will assure us of his continuous and caring love for us.

**The Life of the Church.** As members of his body, the church, we are ever mindful of our duty to recognize God's majesty and to praise him for his continuous concern for us.

The whole Eucharistic Celebration gives glory to God. We single out this duty in a special way on feast days and Sundays as we join our hearts and minds in the liturgical hymn of praise.

> Glory to God in the highest,
>     and peace to his people on earth.
> Lord God, heavenly King,
> almighty God and Father,

we worship you, we give you thanks,
we praise you for your glory.
Lord Jesus Christ, only Son of the Father,
Lord God, Lamb of God,
you take away the sin of the world:
have mercy on us;
you are seated at the right hand of the Father;
receive our prayer.
For you alone are the Holy One,
you alone are the Lord,
you alone are the Most High;
Jesus Christ,
with the Holy Spirit,
in the glory of God the Father. Amen.

## Psalm 147
### Praise God the Maintainer
### of the Universe

At times, people astound us with their kindness and compassion. They graciously respond to
someone in need. They generously share the
gifts with which God has endowed them. Witt-
ingly or not, they are motivated by an awareness
of the infinite goodness of the Lord to his
creatures.

When we pause to count the bountiful blessings of the Lord, we not only want to praise and
thank him, but we are moved to greater generosity toward all who come into our life.

As the psalmist recounts the various gifts of the Lord, his heart bursts forth in praise and thanksgiving. As he mentions the Lord's blessings, the psalm builds to a great crescendo of praise.

It is evident that the poet loves nature because he sees it as a manifestation of God's creating love.

As we pray with the psalmist, we become more and more aware of God's great providence. Our hearts, too, want to sing the glory of God in an everlasting hymn of gratitude and praise.

*Praise the Lord for he is good;*
*sing to our God for he is loving:*
*to him our praise is due.*

*The Lord builds up Jerusalem*
*and brings back Israel's exiles,*
*he heals the broken-hearted,*
*he binds up all their wounds.*
*He fixes the number of the stars;*
*he calls each one by its name.*

*Our Lord is great and almighty;*
*his wisdom can never be measured.*
*The Lord raises the lowly;*
*he humbles the wicked to the dust.*
*O sing to the Lord, giving thanks;*
*sing psalms to our God with the harp.*

*He covers the heavens with clouds;*

*he prepares the rain for the earth,*
*making mountains sprout with grass*
*and with plants to serve man's needs.*
*He provides the beasts with their food*
*and young ravens that call upon him.*

*His delight is not in horses*
*nor his pleasure in warriors' strength.*
*The Lord delights in those who revere him,*
*in those who wait for his love.*

*O praise the Lord, Jerusalem!*
*Zion, praise your God!*

*He has strengthened the bars of your gates,*
*he has blessed the children within you.*
*He established peace on your borders,*
*he feeds you with the finest wheat.*

*He sends out his word to the earth*
*and swiftly runs his command.*
*He showers down snow white as wool,*
*he scatters hoar-frost like ashes.*

*He hurls down hailstones like crumbs.*
*The waters are frozen at his touch;*
*he sends forth his word and it melts them:*
*at the breath of his mouth the waters flow.*

*He makes his word known to Jacob,*
*to Israel his laws and decrees.*
*He has not dealt thus with other nations;*
*he has not taught them his decrees.*

**Reflections.** "Praise the Lord for he is good" is an ongoing invitation to lift our hearts and minds to glorify the Lord. The psalmist continues to enumerate the reasons why we should praise the Lord constantly.

"He heals the broken-hearted. . . ." The Lord is aware of every heartache, pain, or sorrow we endure. His loving touch heals all our wounds and our brokenness.

"He fixes the number of stars; he calls each one by name." The stars respond to his call. "When he calls them they answer, 'Here we are!' shining with joy for their Maker" (Bar 3:25).

"O sing to the Lord, giving thanks." As the psalmist encourages us to praise the Lord constantly, he reminds us of all that the Lord provides.

The Lord sustains all the needy, both man and beast, by providing rain for the earth. Of all the birds, the psalmist singles out the raven whose cawing he hears as a cry to God for food.

Our recognition of God as a provident Father will fill our hearts and voices with praise and thanksgiving. God is not pleased with the proud man who depends on "the strength of the steed and the fleetness of men." The Lord is delighted with the humility and confidence of those who trust in him for all their needs.

In the second portion of the psalm, the author urges us once again to glorify God for his providential love. "He has blessed the children within you. / He established peace on your borders, / he feeds you with finest wheat."

Taking up the refrain of Isaiah, the psalmist reminds us of the power of God's creative word. "He showers down snow . . . scatters hoar-frost . . . hurls down hailstones." These expressions characterize the Hebrew language which speaks of God as personally active in all his creation. They attribute nothing to secondary causes. Such language keeps us ever mindful of God's loving providence. "The waters are frozen at his touch; / he sends forth his word and it melts them: / at the breath of his mouth the waters flow."

**The Life of Jesus.** We have no more perfect model of prayer than Jesus. While on earth, he joined his people regularly in their rituals and prayers. As he sang the psalms, his heart must have rejoiced in praising and glorifying his Father.

Jesus came into the world to proclaim the word of the Father. In fact, he is the very Word of God.

We have reason to praise God because of the power of his word. Jesus tells us it has the power to cleanse. "You are clean already, thanks to the word I have spoken to you" (Jn 15:3).

If we are faithful in keeping the word of God we will certainly hear Jesus saying to us: "I solemnly assure you, / the man who hears my word / and has faith in him who sent me / possesses eternal life" (Jn 5:24).

**The Life of the Church.** In the liturgical prayers of the church, the hymns, psalms, and prayers of praise are generously interspersed. These prayers remind us that our primary task is to render praise and glory to God.

When any psalm is used in the liturgy, it is always concluded with a short doxology: "Glory to the Father, and to the Son, and to the Holy Spirit . . ." This makes every psalm a hymn of praise.

In the Mass, before beginning the Communion Rite, we formally conclude the Eucharistic Prayer with a joyous doxology: "Through him, with him, in him, in the unity of the Holy Spirit, all glory and honor is yours, almighty Father, for ever and ever. Amen."

In the early church, the "Amen" was sung long, loud, and joyously, not only in the church where the celebration was taking place, but also in the streets where the church bells invited the whole city to join in the "Great Amen."

# ELEVEN

# Grand Finale

## *Psalm 150*
## *Standing Ovation*

WE HAVE ALL EXPERIENCED the joy and elation which a good concert can arouse in us. Our hearts want to sing and dance for joy.

Usually such a concert climaxes with a grand finale bringing the audience to its feet with a resounding, appreciative ovation.

We can relive such an experience each time we pray or sing Psalm 150. In this grand finale, the psalmist brings us to our feet with a singing heart and dancing feet as he summons us to proclaim the glory of God.

This is his final invitation to use every available musical instrument, as well as everything that lives and breathes, to give praise to the Lord.

In the Psalter, we discover every form of prayer: petition, sorrow, thanksgiving. We also find instruction, warning, and exhortation.

But throughout all is threaded an invitation

and encouragement to praise and glorify the majestic God of heaven and earth. Praise bursts forth in all the *hallel* psalms, but especially in this final doxology.

Let us join the psalmist as he prays and sings the praise of the Lord.

> *Praise God in his holy place,*
> *praise him in his mighty heavens.*
> *Praise him for his powerful deeds,*
> *praise his surpassing greatness.*
>
> *O praise him with sound of trumpet,*
> *Praise him with lute and harp.*
> *Praise him with timbrel and dance,*
> *praise him with strings and pipes.*
>
> *O praise him with resounding cymbals,*
> *praise him with clashing of cymbals.*
> *Let everything that lives and that breathes*
> *give praise to the Lord.*

**Reflections.** The psalm begins and ends with "alleluia." This is a Hebrew word which comes to us through the Greek and Latin and means "Praise the Lord."

This psalm not only begins and ends with an invitation to praise God, but within its six short verses we are urged eleven times to praise the Lord. The frequent repetition reflects the psalmist's need to give God glory and praise.

The psalmist says we should praise God because of "his powerful deeds and his surpassing greatness." The inspired writer wants the full orchestra to sound the praises of God. He lists all the instruments which were used in the Temple worship.

Praise the Lord "with the sound of trumpet, with lute and harp, with timbrel and dance, with strings and pipes." Not only does he want the resounding praise of a full orchestra, but he also calls for a hymn of praise "with resounding cymbals and with clashing of cymbals."

As we hear this joyous rendition, our own hearts leap with gladness as we join in praising our gracious, loving God.

Finally the psalmist calls upon all creation to sing the praise of the Lord. "Let everything that lives and breathes / give praise to the Lord."

**The Life of Jesus.** Jesus came into the world to give glory to the Father. In his high-priestly prayer, Jesus prays that the Father may be glorified and that he himself may receive glory so that eventually we, too, may receive glory.

Jesus explains how he praised the Father and gave him glory: "I have given you glory on earth / by finishing the work you gave me to do" (Jn 17:4).

The work which Jesus was given to do was our redemption. For this he was glorified, and we have received eternal life.

> Father, the hour has come! / Give glory to your son / that your Son may give glory to you, / inasmuch as you have given him authority over all mankind, / that he may bestow eternal life on those you gave him" (Jn 17:1f).

Jesus explained to us how we could praise the Father by using well the gifts he has given us and by following the way of life which Jesus showed. "My Father has been glorified / in your bearing much fruit / and becoming my disciples" (Jn 15:8).

A disciple praises God by striving to put on the new man—the image of Jesus.

**The Life of the Church.** In the liturgy, the church joyously sings the praises of God. It reminds us that praise is our Christian response for the gift of Jesus manifested in his redemptive power.

Praise is directed more to the person of God, while thanks focuses on his gifts. Praise is more theocentric and is directed to God simply because he is God.

As we praise God we become lost in God. It

draws us into adoration and worship. It can lead into ecstasy.

Praise often becomes thanksgiving and blessing. Praise and thanksgiving evoke the same exterior manifestation of joy, especially in worship.

As Christians, we ascend to God with Christ. He brings us to the Father. As we sing the praise of our Father, it leads us into profound union with God.

With the hosts of heaven let us sing: "O Lord our God, you are worthy / to receive glory and honor and power! / For you have created all things, / by your will they came to be and were made" (Rv 4:11).

Jesus, too, deserves our praise, especially for his redemptive work. "Worthy is the Lamb that was slain to receive power and riches, wisdom and strength, honor and glory and praise" (Rv 5:12).

Together we praise the Father and the Son: "To the One seated on the throne / and to the Lamb / be praise and honor, glory and might, / forever and ever!" (Rv 5:12f).

*Also from Fr. David Rosage*

## Follow Me
A Pocket Guide to Daily Scriptural Prayer
Daily scriptural prayer based on Jesus' own words
from the Gospels. Conveniently sized to fit in a
woman's purse or a man's shirt pocket. Ideal for
the person on the go. $3.95

## Climbing Higher
Reflections for Our Spiritual Journey
Mountains—from Sinai to Calvary—are found
everywhere in God's dealings with his people.
Through his unique reflections on the "mountain
experiences" of the Bible, Fr. David Rosage helps
us to climb the mountains of our daily lives. $4.95

## Speak, Lord, Your Servant Is Listening
A Daily Guide to Scriptural Prayer
Fr. Rosage's original best seller. Over 300,000
copies have been sold! $2.45

Available at your bookstore or from
**Servant Publications ● Dept. 209 ● P.O. Box 7455
● Ann Arbor, Michigan 48107**
Please include payment plus $.75 for postage
*Send for your FREE catalog of Christian books, music, and cassettes.*